DISHING
Hollywood

DISHING

Hollywood

The Real Scoop on Tinseltown's Most Notorious Scandals

laurie jacobson

Cumberland House
Nashville, Tennessee

DISHING HOLLYWOOD

PUBLISHED BY CUMBERLAND HOUSE PUBLISHING

431 Harding Industrial Drive

Nashville, Tennessee 37211

Cover design: Unlikely Suburban Design
Text design: Mary Sanford

Library of Congress Cataloging-in-Publication Data

Jacobson, Laurie.
  Dishing Hollywood : the real scoop on Tinseltown's most notorious scandals / Laurie Jacobson.
       p. cm.
  ISBN 1-58182-370-3 (alk. paper)
  1. Motion picture actors and actresses—United States—Biography. 2. Cookery, American. I. Title.
  PN1998.2.J28 2003
  791.4302'8'092273—dc22

                                                                      2003019059

Printed in the United States of America
  2 3 4 5 6 7—09 08 07

To the memory of my great friend

WILLIAM FRANKLIN,

Whose appetite for life was a constant inspiration,

and to waiters and waitresses everywhere

Contents

Acknowledgments   *ix*

Introduction   *xi*

Breakfast _____ 3

GARY COOPER	Gary Cooper's Buttermilk Griddle Cakes	5
ROMAN POLANSKI	Huevos Rancheros and Tomato-Chipotle Salsa	9
SPADE COOLEY	Grits	15
RIVER PHOENIX	Vegan Tofu Smoothie and Tofu Scrambles	21

Lunch _____ 27

CARL "ALFALFA" SWITZER	Alfalfa's Franks and Beans	29
DEBBIE REYNOLDS	Tacos	33
MONTGOMERY CLIFT	Monty's Goose Liver Sandwich	37
INGER STEVENS	The Inger Stevens BLT with Avocado	41
CASS ELLIOT	Chili Esperanza	47

Cocktails 51

WILLIAM DESMOND TAYLOR	Orange Blossoms	53
THELMA TODD	The Three Finger, A New Old Fashioned, and the Joya	61
CHARLES FARRELL	The Folding Farrell	71
ERROL FLYNN	The Zombie	77
DOROTHY KILGALLEN	Vodka Tonic à la the Regency Hotel	81

Hors D'Oeuvres and Soup and Salad 85

CLARA BOW	Deviled Oysters on the Half Shell	87
THE BLACK DAHLIA	Aunt Betty's Corn Chowder and A "John's" Marinara Sauce	95
BING CROSBY	Ceviche	101
PHIL SPECTOR	Tana Salad	107

Main Dishes 113

CHEIRO	Fricassee of Chicken	115
RUDOLPH VALENTINO	Spaghetti with Mussels	121
MARY ASTOR	Rouladen or Mock Birds	129
CLARA BLANDICK	Auntie Em's Roasted Chicken	133
BENJAMIN "BUGSY" SIEGEL	Grilled Trout Fillets with Olive Oil and Lemon	137
JOAN CRAWFORD	Joan's Meat Loaf	141
ROBERT MITCHUM	Mitchum's Fettuccine Alla Alfredo	145
LANA TURNER	Shrimp Scampi	149
JOHN WAYNE	Cheese Casserole	155
MARILYN MONROE	Scaloppine of Veal	159
FRANK SINATRA	Sinatra's Quick Italian Tomato Sauce	165
SAL MINEO	Linguine with Clams à la Sal	169
SHARON TATE	Cheese Enchiladas	173
LIBERACE	Ham Loaf and Mustard Sauce	179
NATALIE WOOD	Grilled Swordfish	183
NICOLE BROWN SIMPSON	Nicole's Last Supper	189
ROBERT BLAKE	Fusilli e Minestra alla Robert Blake	193

Side Dishes 199

LUPE VELEZ	Spanish Rice and Refried Beans	201
DAVID NIVEN	Red Rice Mold	207
BOBBY DARIN	Special Spinach	211

Desserts 215

CAROLE LANDIS	Lemon Chiffon Pie	217
GEORGE REEVES	Superman Cookies	225
JEAN SEBERG	Macaroon Peaches	229
DIANE LINKLETTER	Diane's Sugar Cookies	233
DIVINE	Caramel Flan	239

Bibliography	*245*
Picture Credits	*247*
Index	*249*

Acknowledgments

To Brent Farris for whetting my appetite. . . .

To my husband, Jon Provost, for his patience, support, and nourishment.

To my brother, Mark Jacobson, for his generous "second helping."

To Marc Wanamaker, my partner in crime.

To Tony Oleshansky for all the years.

And for their unrestrained assistance: Arnoldo Archila, Warren Beath, Mike Caffey, Jonn G. Christian, Estella Collier, Benny Drinnon, Jenna Girard, Lisa Houston, Janice Knowlton, Patrick Langdon, Cassie Marple, Mom, Nada Palikovic, James R. Parish, William T. Patterson, Mary Sanford, Rudy Schafer, Brad Schreiber, Greg Smith, Frank Smoot, Carrie Snow, Jan Wahl.

Introduction

Lives tragically cut short, unsolved mysteries, dramatic suicides, steamy affairs—Tinseltown serves them up in generous portions. The town's full of tales like that; always has been, always will. The town is also full of people who pay big dough or pull strings to make sure certain details of those stories never reach the light of day. But they always surface eventually . . . if you know where to look. I've been writing about Hollywood for close to twenty-five years. I got the straight scoop. But stick around, I got more than that. Pull up a chair, bring your appetite, and get it while it's hot, kiddo.

Hollywood's bright lights sometimes hide the darkness . . . in the corners, around the edges. A lot of people end up there. When it happens to a celebrity, it's front-page news. For some, reading about it just isn't enough. They want to taste it—literally. Since making the news as the restaurant where Robert Blake's wife ate before she was shot to death, business at Vitello's has increased 25 percent. When reporters retraced the last hours of Nicole Brown Simpson's life, including where she ate supper, curious citizens descended on Mezzaluna restaurant like a plague of locusts, copping matchbooks and menus and all ordering her last meal. Mezzaluna folded under all the attention. Vitello's—they named a dish after Blake. You see, they recognize that romance, scandal, and murder can really work up an appetite. *Dishing Hollywood* serves up the real scoop on more than forty juicy scandals with a recipe connected to each one: last suppers, first dates, favorite dishes—stories with some real meat to them.

Some names here you may not know—that's part of the reason I picked them. Spade Cooley was never what you'd call a household name, but his trial for murder was the talk of Hollywood in '61. And Cheiro predicted the fortunes and failures for most of European and Hollywood royalty—on the level. Other names are here because they capture a moment in time: Jean Seberg, the Black Panthers, and the FBI: Hoover destroyed her. Liberace and the AIDS crisis: the coroner stopped his funeral. And Dorothy Kilgallen and the JFK conspiracy: she told friends she had big news and woke up dead.

Hollywood is full of sad stories about beautiful women. The two I thought would be the most obvious turned out to be the most interesting. Lupe Velez was a talented tomato, most remembered for drowning in the crapper in the suicide-gone-wrong of all time. And the crapper is just where *that* story belongs. Carole Landis—Hollywood, her husband, and Rex Harrison all left her behind, and she checked out permanently. What's news about that? Plenty. I got information that will make you see those dark final hours in a whole new light. And that ain't all: Inger Stevens's "suicide" looks more and more like murder. Mama Cass—the ham sandwich was baloney! Divine . . . what she ate that final night would have given most people a heart attack, but fifteen years later, we now learn the real cause.

A few stories you think you've heard before, but you don't know the half of it, friend. You wanna know who killed the Black Dahlia? Her murder has never been solved, but I know who did it, and I have a recipe she used to whip up for the girl who witnessed her grisly end. Nobody has a recipe from the Black Dahlia. You think you know the whole story about Errol Flynn's trial for rape? I have the whole story: the plane waiting at the airport, the second payoff . . . and Flynn's favorite drink from Don the Beachcomber's.

Did you know that every August 8, Sharon Tate fans go to L.A.'s El Coyote restaurant? That night in 1969, Sharon ate dinner there. She was murdered by the Manson gang hours later. So much has been written about that infamous night, but nobody ever said what she ate. I went looking and got more than I hoped for. I found her favorite waitress from El Coyote . . . and happy moments they shared that night.

Sharon's widower, director Roman Polanski, got in deep in an ugly mess in 1977. A longtime friend of mine and a lifetime waitress made him forget his troubles, if just for a moment—before bringing him his last meal in America.

Now, I'm no cook, but even *I* recognize that the recipes themselves have a lot to say. One's over a hundred years old and involves catching the chicken and scaring it into being tender. The rest span eighty-five years, complete with obsolete brand names and weird ingredients, like suet. Rudolph Valentino's recipe for spaghetti and mussels is so simple, it's positively modern. Mary Astor's Rouladen . . . what the hell is *Rouladen* anyway?

These recipes for scandal begin with breakfast, then go on to cocktails and appetizers, all the way through to dessert. Some you'll never make, but the stories are enough to satisfy your appetite. Others are fun and delicious, just like the scoop that goes with them. Think of it this way. If you had a nice plate, people would say, "That's a nice plate." If you had a nice plate that was Natalie Wood's, people would say, "Really?! How'd you get it? Where did it come from? When did she use it?" See what I mean? So picture this: theme parties with Clara Bow's deviled oysters and the sex that ruined her career; Charlie Farrell's hangover cure—one of the most popular drinks in the world; Sinatra's pasta sauce and the story of his "wrong-door raid"; Lana Turner's scampi and her hoodlum homicide; Marilyn and Joltin' Joe's first-date-supper; Bobby Darin's spinach fixed by his mother, no wait, his sister, no wait. . . . George Reeves's cookies didn't help him dodge that speeding bullet. . . . Serve these and the dinner conversation is built in: Everyone will be dishing the dish.

So quit stallin' and see what looks good on the menu. And don't forget to tip your waitress.

LAURIE JACOBSON, FORMER WAITRESS
SUMMER 2003

"Two things I can smell inside a hundred feet: burning hamburger and romance."

OUT OF THE PAST, 1947

DISHING
Hollywood

Breakfast

Gary Cooper 5

Roman Polanski 9

Spade Cooley 15

River Phoenix 21

"Run along to Ito and tell him to bring me a light breakfast—black coffee and a Monkey Gland. Oh, oh. And a cold towel for your Auntie Vera."

AUNTIE MAME, 1958

Gary Cooper

A lot of things have been said about Gary Cooper . . . and most of them by women.

"Gary has the biggest one in town," said kiss-and-tell star Lupe Velez.

"He was hung like a horse and could go all night long, the best," recalled the Roaring Twenties' "IT" girl, Clara Bow. And she ought to know. Her appetite for sex left more than one man begging for mercy. She nicknamed Cooper "Studs." Clara was crazy about him and did a lot to help his career. He was just another cowboy actor until she got him the flyboy role in *Wings*. For Coop, a boy who was close to his mother, the free-spirited Clara was a little slice of heaven.

Gary's beloved mom was a hoity-toity English dame. Gary and his brother lived with her in England the first half of their lives, then with both parents on a Montana ranch. The cowboy bit was no act—he was born to it. Six-foot-three, 170 pounds, brown hair, blue eyes, large hands, lanky, leggy, trim, soft-spoken, a Midwestern drawl tinged with a

Above: Dishing with Evelyn Brent in the Paramount Commisary.

British accent, long-faced, long-necked, long, long, LONG! He spoke in one- or two-word sentences—what you call the strong, silent type. Mama Cooper didn't think her son would stand a chance in Hollywood against all those wild women, so she followed him there.

Gossip maven Hedda Hopper said she thought Gary was attracted to Clara Bow and Lupe Velez because they were the direct opposite of his mother. Coop was nuts for Clara and popped the question. Clara adored him, but turned him down. Mom would have

Vertical or horizontal, Coop was legendary.

killed him if she'd known. She did put an end to his romance with the wild and lusty Velez. And brother, that was some fire she put out. Latin Lupe was a beautiful, passionate pepper. What a temper. But she made up for it between the sheets. What a woman. Cooper was over the moon for her, and for Lupe, it was true love. She dropped crooner Russ Columbo like a hot tamale for Gary. Hollywood's red hot couple were photographed everywhere together, and the fan magazines were filled with stories of their romance, including foolish public fights the tempestuous Velez was known for. Mama Cooper couldn't stand it anymore. She packed his bags and put him on the next train out of town. Lupe caught him leaving and ran through the station waving a gun, screaming, "Gareee, you son of a beetch!" She fired. He ducked, hopped on board, and slammed the door. Lupe later said she thought he was the most humble, caring, sensitive man she had ever known, "but he was controlled by his mother."

Mama's boy or not, women found him irresistible. One who did, Ingrid Bergman, said, "Every woman who met Gary was in love with him." His jaw-dropping good looks and bedroom prowess became the stuff of legend. When asked why she was leaving Broadway for Hollywood, flamboyant Tallulah Bankhead replied without hesitation, "To f--- that di-VINE Gary Cooper." (When reminded of this years later, Tallu drawled, "Mission accomplished.") Coop truly adored women and strove to make them happy. He seemed to know instinctively what they wanted. "Gary made every woman feel like she was the only woman in the world," Joan Crawford said. He was not faithful to any, sometimes seeing two or three at the same time. During Hollywood's glamorous age, he made love to the most beautiful women in the world: Carole Lombard, Bergman, Grace Kelly, Merle Oberon, Bow, Velez, and Patricia Neal, who called him "the most gorgeously attractive man." Typically for Gary, when the

Coop and Mom at his first TV appearance, August '55 (with my uncle, PR man Harry Friedman).

movie was done, so was the affair. But while it lasted, it was first-class loving. Gary's life was the stuff of headlines. But he paid no attention to the gossip. He was his own man . . . and his mother's.

"I don't think I've ever drunk champagne before breakfast before. With breakfast on several occasions, but never before, before."
BREAKFAST AT TIFFANY'S, 1961

Actor Richard Arlen sees it another way: "Coop was a mystery; that's one reason women fell for him. He wasn't quoted as saying much so he was a mystery to his fans. He let you figure out for yourself who he was." Yeah, that's it—he was a mystery.

You might think men would be wary of Coop, but damned if they didn't love him too. He was such a great guy, they didn't even envy him for being the nation's top wage earner in 1939. And the public made that happen by seeing all his movies. Coop spoke to them in a way most other actors never could. Strong, humble, soft-spoken, he was a quiet hero and undeniably American. "Until I came along all the leading men were handsome," Coop said, "but luckily they wrote a lot of stories about the fellow next door."

"That fellow, Gary Cooper, is the world's greatest actor," said John Barrymore, considered one of the greats himself. "He can do, with no effort, what the rest of us spend years trying to learn: to be perfectly natural."

Coop won two Oscars and was nominated for a couple more, but that wasn't enough. The Academy wanted to present him with a special, career-achievement Academy Award in 1961, but Coop, a lifetime smoker, was too ill to pick it up. Old pal Jimmy Stewart collected it for him with a tear in his eye. Coop died a month later and Hollywood mourned the loss of a one-of-a-kind: a man's man, a ladies' man, and an Everyman.

Gary borrowed this recipe from his mom, of course. The griddle cakes were a fixture of the Cooper ranch in Montana.

Gary Cooper's Buttermilk Griddle Cakes

1	cup buttermilk
½	cup sweet cream
1	egg, well beaten
1	teaspoon baking soda
½	teaspoon salt
1	tablespoon melted butter
2	tablespoons granulated cornmeal
2	cups flour

In a large bowl mix the ingredients in the order given. Drop by spoonfuls on a greased hot griddle. Cook on one side, and when puffed, full of bubbles, and well-cooked on edges, turn and cook on the other side. Serve with butter and maple syrup. Griddle cakes from buttermilk have an unusually good flavor and are "tenderer" (according to Coop himself) than those made from plain milk or water.

Roman Polanski

Roman Polanski's father sneaked him to the edge of the Krakow ghetto, snipped the barbed wire, and pushed him through. He was ten years old, alone, and terrified, yet somehow he survived on his own in Nazi-occupied Poland until the end of the war. Roman and his dad were reunited after the war, but the rest of his family perished in the death camps. Roman was deeply traumatized, and his father tried everything to reach him, finally sending him to acting school. Theater games helped bring him out of his shell and to his destiny as one of the cinema's most controversial directors.

Polanski enjoyed professional success, but personal happiness was another story. In 1969, while he was filming in London, deranged followers of Charles Manson broke into his home and savagely murdered his young wife, actress Sharon Tate, their unborn son, and three close friends. The media kicked him when he was down, implying that his wife and friends were responsible for their own deaths because they lived a degenerate, drug-

The Fearless Vampire Killers:
Roman and Sharon falling in love.

oriented, hippie lifestyle. Polanski's films, in particular *Rosemary's Baby,* proved it. Only a weirdo could make a movie like that. Yeah, that was it—the foreign squirt was a creep. The label stuck like glue.

Films like *Repulsion, Rosemary's Baby,* and *Chinatown* contain elements of Polanski's terrifying childhood: isolation, violence, sexual deviation. But his most personal film, his masterpiece, *The Pianist,* is a stunning depiction of the Holocaust through the eyes of a Polish pianist hiding from the Nazis. In 2002, it received seven Oscar nominations, including Best Picture, but Polanski couldn't make the show. If he sets foot in this country, he goes directly to jail.

The whispers about Polanski returned to hang him in 1977. He was arrested on charges of drugging and raping a thirteen-year-old model at Jack Nicholson's place. While reporting the details of this latest scandal, newspapers enthusiastically dredged up the rumors of drugs, orgies, and black magic that had surrounded his wife's murder.

Jokes circled the globe. "Did you hear Polanski is making a new film? *Close Encounters with the Third Grade.*" But Polanski was not laughing. A grand jury indicted him on six charges. Afterward, during meetings in the judge's chambers, the more serious charges were dropped.

Dino De Laurentiis rushed Polanski into preproduction on his next film. The director made all of his court appearances, and the Hollywood-savvy judge worked with the film's production schedule, even allowing Polanski to travel to Europe. When the judge determined that Polanski had to serve prison time at Chino for psychiatric testing, the director surrendered early and did forty-two days.

In 1978, the victim's lawyer, Polanski's attorney, and the district attorney's office came to an agreement for a plea bargain that was acceptable to everyone, including the victim and her family. But before sentencing, the judge openly discussed the case with influential pals at his country club. They criticized him for whitewashing the crime and pressured him to throw the book at this pervert. After some flip-flopping, the judge held a press conference to announce his plans to prevent Polanski from ever living and working in the United States again. He'd never consider the plea bargain. Rather than take the fall, Polanski fled the country.

The judge was gung ho to sentence him in absentia, but Polanski's attorneys prevented him from doing so with a "statement of disqualification." They claimed extreme bias and the impossibility of an impartial hearing from him. Even the opposing counsel endorsed it. The judge stepped down "for the sake of expediency."

If Polanski ever returns to the United States, he will immediately be arrested and held without bail. His victim, now thirty-nine, has asked that he be allowed to return and live freely. At the time of his nominations for *The Pianist,* she told the *L.A. Times,* "I don't have any hard feelings toward him, or any sympathy."

Apparently, Hollywood decided all was forgiven, too. *The Pianist* scored Oscars for Ronald Harwood (Best Original Screenplay) and Adrien Brody (Best Actor). And the room

"I'd like an omelet, plain, and a chicken salad sandwich on wheat toast, no mayonnaise, no butter, no lettuce. And a cup of coffee."

"A #2: chicken salad sand. Hold the butter, the lettuce, the mayo. And a cup of coffee. Anything else?"

"Yeah, now all you have to do is hold the chicken, bring me the toast, give me a check for the chicken salad sandwich, and you haven't broken any rules."

"You want me to hold the chicken, huh?"

"I want you to hold it between your knees."

FIVE EASY PIECES, 1970

erupted with gasps and applause, rising to its collective feet, when Harrison Ford announced the Oscar for Best Director: Roman Polanski.

During the trial, Polanski stayed at the Beverly Wilshire Hotel. One morning, he rushed into Hernando's Hideaway, one of the hotel's restaurants. He was more than a little distracted. Waitress Cassie Marple approached him for his order. Before he could speak, she did.

"We have something in common."

"Oh really?" he sneered. "What could that possibly be?"

"I was Jay Sebring's mother-in-law."

Sebring had been the first in the house to die at the hands of the Manson family, defending Sharon. Cassie's daughter Cami had married and divorced Jay, but he'd stayed close with them. He was that kind of guy. Sharon had broken off her engagement to Jay when she met Roman, but Jay had remained devoted and came to love Roman too. He'd been a special friend. Polanski melted instantly. He embraced Cassie and they spoke warmly of Jay. For a moment, all his problems were forgotten; but only for a moment. Then, patting her hand, he said, "My dear, bring me huevos rancheros in a hurry."

Hours later, the press reported that Polanski hopped a plane to Europe. Cassie served him his last meal in America . . . until further notice.

Huevos Rancheros

4 servings

1	to 2 tablespoons vegetable oil
4	corn tortillas
8	eggs

Salt and ground black
pepper to taste
Tomato-Chipotle Salsa
(see below)

In a large, nonstick skillet heat the vegetable oil over medium high heat. When hot, add the corn tortillas one at a time and quick-fry for 2 to 3 seconds on each side. Remove the tortillas to paper towels to drain, then wrap in foil and keep warm in a 200° oven.

Reduce the heat to medium low (use two skillets if the eggs will not all fit at once) and add a bit more oil if needed. Break the eggs into the skillet. Let cook until set, sunny-side-up. Cover the pan for a minute or so for the most even cooking. Season with salt and pepper to taste.

Set a tortilla on each of 4 warmed plates and top with 2 eggs. Spoon a generous ½ cup of the warm Tomato-Chipotle Salsa around each serving.

Serve immediately sprinkled with finely crumbled Mexican queso fresco, "farmer cheese," or feta cheese and chopped fresh cilantro.

Tomato-Chipotle Salsa

6	medium, ripe tomatoes, halved
1	small onion, finely chopped
¼	cup coarsely chopped fresh cilantro
3	tablespoons fresh lime juice
2	tablespoons olive oil
2	cloves garlic, finely chopped
1½	teaspoons finely chopped canned chipotle pepper
1	teaspoon cumin
	Salt to taste

Place the tomatoes on a grill or broiler pan. Grill or broil as close to the heat as possible until the skin is blackened and blistered, about 5 minutes on each side. When you can handle them, peel the skin and chop coarsely. Place in a mixing bowl and add the remaining ingredients. Serve immediately. These eggs are usually accompanied with refried beans.

Spade Cooley

Spade Cooley was dealt a pretty bleak hand. It was the fiddle that saved him—saved him, hell, it made him famous . . . but paying the fiddler brought him down, way down: to booze, pills, and a murder so gruesome, you couldn't stand to know the whole story.

Donnell Cooley was born dirt-poor in the Oklahoma Dust Bowl to a mother, cold and mean, and a "half-breed" drunk of a father who gambled away what little the family had. Only good thing he ever did was play the fiddle. Donnell loved it, had a natural instinct. He was so good that at thirteen he was sent to an Indian school for the musically gifted. Gambling with friends there earned him the nickname Spade.

He followed his cowboy heroes of the silver screen to Hollywood, land of opportunity. He hung around Republic Studios until he screwed up the courage to sneak onto Gene Autry's set. He got caught, but man, the guy played a crazy fiddle. And he looked so much like Roy Rogers they could've been brothers. Autry made the introduction, and

Rogers hired Spade as his stand-in and stuntman. In '36, Rogers finally made him the featured fiddle player in his group, Riders of the Purple Sage.

By '42, Spade had his own band with a new and different sound—Western Swing, they called it: big band with a touch of country. L.A. loved Spade. He played a record-breaking seventy-four weeks straight at the Venice Pier Ballroom and got offered a recording contract. Success meant money . . . and women and drinkin' and chain-smokin'— and lots of women. Spade might have only been 5'4" and 125 pounds soaking wet, but he was *tall* in the saddle, if you get my drift. He wore real tight pants, danced in a crude sexual manner, and let's say women at the foot of the stage did not look up to see his face. Right about then, he penned his first big hit; it would also be his epitaph: "Shame, Shame on You."

"Meet me down in the bar! We'll drink breakfast together."
THE BIG BROADCAST OF 1938

Cooley went to hell in a fast car. He was livin' the high life, literally, wearing six-inch heels on his fancy cowboy boots. He drank Jack Daniel's and ate Benzedrine for breakfast. For Spade, the '40s were a haze of hookers, bandstand bimbos, and a lot of "disturbing the peace" charges. All the cops knew Spade. His "never-say-no" policy to play benefits for families of fallen cops had raised a lot of dough. The chief of police was a close pal. Spade had a permanent "get out of jail free" card.

Women—Spade couldn't get enough. His poor wife waited, sometimes days, for him to come home to her and their son. He was busy holding Monday night singer "auditions." Seems he was always looking for a new singer. The band took bets and kept notes. He had fifty women a week seventy-five times . . . mostly blondes in their late teens. That's how he met his second wife, Ella Mae, except he totally flipped for her. She couldn't sing a lick, but she was pretty, and you had to be blind not to see they were stupid in love. She sang with the band for six months, but guys gawking at her made him sore. He "retired" her and they married in 1945.

Cooley moved to headliner status at the high-class Santa Monica Ballroom on the pier. He sang in a handful of movies, his records sold like hotcakes, and in 1948 TV came calling. *The Spade Cooley Show* debuted on the West Coast and within a few months, it was hogging 75 percent of the audience. Broadcast live from the Santa Monica Ballroom, Cooley's show had a guest list that read like a "who's who" of Hollywood: Clark Gable, Sammy Davis, Sinatra, Autry, Ronald Reagan. "Spade Cooley's formula for a show with top musical entertainment, a dash of western flavor, and a good sprinkling of comedy has proven to be just what the viewers ordered," said *TV Guide.* The runt half-breed became a multimillionaire. He and Ella Mae had two kids. But his bad habits got worse: drinking, drugging, endless women. Cooley beat a statutory rape charge—the cops were his pals, remember? But nobody could save him from a bad investment. He sank seven million and more into a real-estate venture and lost everything. Wound tighter than a top on bennies, Cooley became unpredictable, violent, and out of control. It was scary just being around the guy. The network fired him.

Drugs had made him crazy, psychotic, paranoid. Somehow, he got it into his fool head that sweet Ella Mae had been sleeping with Roy Rogers for ten years. Of course, it wasn't true. No matter how brutally or savagely he hit her, it would never be true. But he couldn't stop trying to get her to admit it: teeth knocked loose, eyes swollen shut, lips split, ribs broken, road burn and worse. In March of '61, he went on a rampage. For twenty-one days, he drove her from motel to motel where he was sure she'd been with Roy. When she finally showed up at Cooley's manager's, Bobbie Bennett barely recognized her. Bobbie begged her to call the cops. "Nothing can stop him, not even God," Ella Mae told her. "He's going to kill me and my beloved husband doesn't even know it, let alone how to stop himself. Don't make trouble or he'll kill you too and anyone who gets in his way. That's just the way things are now." She and Spade were going home to work things out. That's the last time Bobbie saw her alive.

Bobbie told the story two decades later to writer Jonn G. Christian. "Those were her exact words. I'll never forget that girl's incredible tranquillity when she told me that. . . . Spade was the sickest, most pathetic man I'd ever seen. It was tearing me apart seeing that man reduced to some kind of Frankenstein monster—all those pills and booze, all this stuff on top of his financial mess."

Spade called Bobbie five nights later and told her to come out to the ranch. When she got there, the house was quiet and all the lights were off, inside and out. A madman opened the door. Spade was covered in blood, his hands swollen and split open. He looked like a skeleton. It was obvious he hadn't eaten for days. Bobbie was terrified. He held a shotgun and motioned her inside with the barrel.

The house was in shambles. Most of the furniture had been reduced to kindling. Blood was everywhere. Bobbie fought back nausea, her heart pounding. He babbled incoherently, something about Ella Mae being asleep. She didn't want to do anything that might set him off. Where were the children? With family. Where was Ella Mae? Sleeping. Spade said Ella Mae had had a bad fall. Bobbie glanced toward the master bath and saw the glass shower door broken outward. Spade led her down the blood-spattered hallway to the bedroom. Ella Mae was on the bed, wrapped in a blanket, a few blonde hairs protruding from the top. Bobbie reached to stroke them and choked back a scream; they were not attached. She opened the blanket. Ella Mae was naked. She'd been dead for hours and was already stiff. The damage Spade inflicted left her body almost unrecognizable. Believe me, friend, you don't want the details.

At the trial, Cooley's fourteen-year-old daughter, Melody, testified she had witnessed part of her mother's murder. She told the jurors her father dragged her mother through the house by her hair, pounded her head on the floor, stomped on her stomach, and burned her with cigarettes when she wouldn't get up. He said if she told, he'd kill her too. Melody tried to revive her mom. When she couldn't, she ran for her life. You could have heard a pin drop in that courtroom. All eyes were on Cooley. He seemed dazed, disoriented. He didn't testify. It took the jury five minutes to reach a verdict. Killing by torture. The sentence: life in prison.

Without the liquor and pills, Spade's mental problems cleared up in jail, but shame and guilt aged him considerably, not to mention a heart condition. So after just eight years—the minimum time to serve for a life sentence—Cooley being a model prisoner with friends in high places and all, the powers that be said he could go. But the boys in blue couldn't wait. A few months before his release date, they wanted to throw the guy a big party at a sheriffs' fundraiser in Oakland, California. Only one man could make that happen—let a prisoner out before the minimum time served: the governor, Ronald Reagan. Ronnie didn't hesitate before signing the bill for his old pal.

When Cooley got to the Oakland Arena, he dropped his socks. Forty uniformed cops formed a welcoming committee. Lifelong pal Chill Wills cried, hugged him, and pushed him toward a cheering throng. Spade picked out Jack Benny, Hop-A-Long Cassidy, Duke Wayne, Gene Autry, Johnny Cash, Lucy and Desi, James Garner. He was speechless.

"Most of these men all knew that Spade didn't mean to kill Ella Mae," said Bobbie. "They knew he'd gone insane from all the drinking and drugs and his real-estate situation . . . they knew Spade and Ella Mae loved and worshiped each other. They knew it well."

A fancy cowboy suit and his beloved fiddle were waiting for him. So was nearly every musician from his band in the last twenty-five years. NBC-TV was filming the whole thing. Spade began to fiddle and the crowd went wild. He gave it everything he had, played twenty minutes of go-crazy stuff non-stop.

> "When did you last see your husband?"
> "At breakfast."
> "Did you talk to him?"
> "Sure, I asked him to pass me the salt."
> AFFAIR IN TRINIDAD, 1952

Cops were dancing in the aisles . . . with their wives. Chill Wills called intermission and Spade left the stage to thunderous applause.

His cowboy suit was soaked through. In his dressing room, he smoked a cigarette and downed two Cokes in three minutes, trying to cool down. He opened his fiddle case and pulled back the lining. The picture of Ella Mae and the kids was still there. He took it out.

Chill Wills came to get him. "Ya ready, Spade? They're waitin'." No reply. He tried the door, but something was blocking it—Spade. He was dead; the son of a bitch had had a heart attack. Just then, the band began to play: "Shame, Shame on You."

Spade Cooley loved to sit down to a cowboy's breakfast.

Grits

1	teaspoon salt
5	cups water
1	cup grits
	Butter or grated Cheddar cheese

Bring the salted water to a boil. Stir in the grits. Cover and cook, stirring occasionally, over low heat until thick, about 20 minutes. Serve hot with butter or grated Cheddar cheese.

"Hot cakes and coffee . . . is that all?"

"No, but the rest isn't on the menu."

"You couldn't afford it if it was."

I WAKE UP SCREAMING, 1941

River Phoenix

It just didn't make sense. This was not just another kid actor screwing up on drugs. This was about the very best actor of his generation making a terrible mistake and losing it all. He was smart, compassionate, and had so much to give. He was young, gorgeous, and mature beyond his years, with talent in both barrels. Critics called his work "extraordinary," "intense," and "genuine." Director Sidney Lumet said, "He had the face of a fawn, or some magical forest creature." He'd have liked that. A dedicated animal rights activist and environmentalist, River was a vegan—he would not eat meat or dairy. Known for his adamant stand on pure living, he once yelled at costar Christine Lahti for drinking a Diet Coke. The boy was so careful about what he put in or on his body that he turned down lucrative commercials for jeans just because they had leather pieces on the back pockets. Harrison Ford worked on two films with River. "He always stood for something," he told the press after his death. While most members of his generation were photographed mak-

Fans' grief and love spilled out onto the sidewalk where River died.

ing the scene, clubbing, or in rehab, River used his spare time to make public service announcements, speak at local schools, and fundraise for PETA—People for the Ethical Treatment of Animals.

"If I have some celebrity, I hope I can use it to make a difference. The true social reward is that I can speak my mind and share my thoughts about the environment and civilization itself." He was a model of vulnerability, clean living, and professional dedication—James Dean without the angst. He insisted he was living true to his beliefs, but soon the world would know the truth. And the world was shocked—shocked and devastated.

River was born in 1970 in Oregon in a log cabin to bohemian '60s wanderers—strict vegetarians, the whole bit. When River was two, his parents carried him to South America, where they served as missionaries for Children of God, a controversial religious sect now called The Family. They had four more children in four different countries, then moved to Los Angeles and changed their name to Phoenix.

In Hollywood, all the Phoenix children were encouraged to get into movies. Seven-year-old River got work in television right away. By the time he was ten, he was supporting the whole family. Gifted, startlingly mature, with soft, sensitive looks, the kid was a standout from the average teen heartthrob. His big break came in 1986, playing a good kid from the wrong side of the tracks in *Stand by Me.* Two years later, Phoenix received an Oscar nomination for his poignant performance as the son of '60s radicals-on-the-run

Fantasy . . .

. . . and reality.

The Viper Room shut down and posted this sign after River's death.

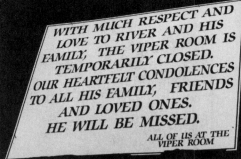

WITH MUCH RESPECT AND LOVE TO RIVER AND HIS FAMILY, THE VIPER ROOM IS TEMPORARILY CLOSED. OUR HEARTFELT CONDOLENCES TO ALL HIS FAMILY, FRIENDS AND LOVED ONES. HE WILL BE MISSED.
ALL OF US AT THE VIPER ROOM

in *Running on Empty*. It should have been the first of many. Instead, it was the one and only. *L.A. Times* film critic Kenneth Turan wrote: "Thinking of his work (in *Running on Empty*), especially of his emotional scenes with Martha Plimpton, and knowing that this is all we are going to get is enough to make you weep."

The twenty-three-year-old made more than a dozen films. But his performance as a narcoleptic hustler in *My Own Private Idaho* in '91 seemed to be a turning point. The seedy, drug-dominated world of the film made quite an impression. His appearance took a dive. His friends changed. Rumors flew that he was using hard drugs. But nobody really bought it, given his clean lifestyle. River was not a regular on the club scene or with the Brat Pack; he didn't even live in L.A. But in October of '93, he was there making a film.

The destination for the evening of October 30 was Johnny Depp's Viper Room, a small Sunset Strip club featuring live music. River planned to play a few numbers with his sister Rain and their band, Aleka's Attic. River's girlfriend, Samantha Mathis, and brother Joaquin came along.

Around 1:00 A.M. Halloween morning, River was getting high with friends in the club's bathroom. Someone offered him high-grade heroin. River snorted it and right away started to shake. He screamed at his friend. He threw up. Something was going terribly wrong. Someone splashed cold water on his face and gave him a Valium to bring him down. Nothing helped. He staggered into the bar and over to Samantha and Rain. "I can't breathe," he said and passed out cold. He came to a couple of minutes later, and the girls and Joaquin dragged him outside.

River collapsed on the sidewalk in front of the club. That's when the seizures started, horrible, violent seizures that wracked his whole body. Photog-rapher Ron Davis was there. "He looked like a fish out of water," said Davis, "thrashing spasmodically, his head flopping from side to side, arms flailing wildly." Rain threw herself on top of him. Davis flagged a cop. People walked by. Cars passed. Joaquin placed a frantic call to 911. Eight minutes went by. The seizures stopped; River was still. When the paramedics arrived at 1:14 A.M., he was in full cardiac arrest. ER physicians did everything to revive him, even inserting a pacemaker, but they could not bring him back. He was pronounced dead at 1:51 A.M.

On Monday morning, the *Los Angeles Times* screamed the question we all asked: *WHY?* Not why did he die . . . why River Phoenix?

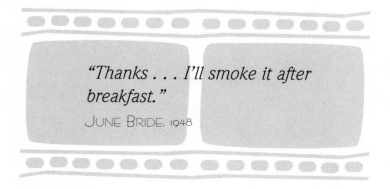

"*Thanks . . . I'll smoke it after breakfast.*"
JUNE BRIDE, 1948

River used to start his days with a smoothie and tofu scrambles. He ended them with heroin. A hard lesson learned much too early.

Vegan Tofu Smoothie

1   banana
6   frozen strawberries
1   cup orange juice
½   cup firm tofu
     Honey (optional)

In a blender or food processor blend all of the ingredients until smooth.

River's mom used to make this dish on the set of River's films for everyone.

Tofu Scrambles

The basic scramble includes chopped green onions and chilies. Tomatoes, mushrooms, salsa, olives, artichokes, or soy strips can be added on request.

Lunch

Carl "Alfalfa" Switzer...29

Debbie Reynolds 33

Montgomery Clift 37

Inger Stevens 41

Cass Elliot 47

Carl "Alfalfa" Switzer

There weren't a lot of tears shed for Carl "Alfalfa" Switzer. He may have been a lovable "Little Rascal" on the screen, but real life was a very different story. Nobody could stand the guy . . . even as a kid. He had an attitude right from the beginning. He often kept the entire *Our Gang* cast and crew waiting for him on the set; he ruined class time for the rest of the kids with relentless, obnoxious behavior; and he played jokes, lots of practical jokes. Fishhooks in Spanky McFarland's back pockets required stitches. Pissing on thousand-watt bulbs caused a stench that cleared the soundstage while costing Hal Roach thousands. Yeah, that Alfalfa was a regular laugh riot. So when the *Our Gang* series came to an end, it's no surprise Carl could not find work. He had two things working against him: nobody liked him and everybody hated him.

He haunted the casting offices and landed a few bit parts, but nothing that paid the bills. To support himself, he worked a variety of odd jobs, usually as a bartender or hunting guide for the likes of Roy Rogers and Henry Fonda. He was convicted and fined for stealing trees from the Sequoia National Forest and selling them for Christmas trees. Frustration was getting the better of him. He was living hand-to-mouth, and humble pie left a bitter taste. He was arrested for drunk and disorderly conduct. He drank more, got tossed out of more bars, made more enemies. He was even shot at as he stood outside a San Fernando Valley bar. A hothead with a drinking problem . . . these things never end well.

Carl's problems with the bottle started early.

It was January 1959. The new year wasn't looking too rosy for Alfalfa. And it got worse fast: Three weeks into it, he was dead. But not everybody agrees on what happened. The official version says Alfie and a pal, Jack Piott, were drinking pretty heavily. Alf had borrowed and lost a hunting dog that belonged to Bud Stiltz; cost him fifty bucks to get it back. On this drunken night, Alf decided to collect the dough from Stiltz. He and Piott went over there and started brawling. They crashed a clock over his head, and Stiltz shot off a round from his .38, sending his wife, Rita, and her three children running. Alf charged at Stiltz with a hunting knife and Stiltz shot him. Justifiable homicide. The end.

Rita's son, Tom Corrigan, son of "Crash" Corrigan, was fourteen at the time. When asked about the official version, he says, "They never tell it right." In a recent interview, Tom says Alf had only a

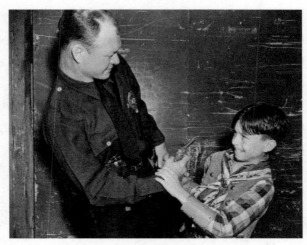

Life would later imitate art for the child star.

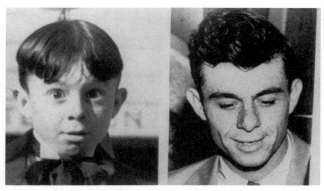

Recipe for disaster: Take one jerk, add heaping helpings of bitterness, booze, and some say speed. Whip to a frenzy.

small penknife in his hand, and it was closed at that. He did not believe his stepfather had to shoot.

Stiltz himself told the story several different ways: that Alf was there to collect a loan and a fight developed; that he threw Alf in a closet and he came out, knife drawn, shouting, "I'm going to kill you"; that Alfalfa ran to the car for his knife; that Alfalfa threw the knife at him . . . you get the picture. And there's more. . . .

Some say there wasn't even a dog.

> "I liked it, Mom, tasted kind of like chicken."
> "It was chicken."
>
> THE WINDOW, 1949

Some say you have only to look at Alfalfa that last year to see he was using drugs. That's what the drive-by shooting was about, not a random attempt. And that's what this argument was about, not Spot but speed.

Whatever way you tell it, Carl Switzer was dead at thirty-two and his lousy disposition was to blame. Anger, booze, meth, unemployment, resentment, fear . . . what a cookie full of arsenic. He was running straight toward the end of the line. Instead, it came up to meet him.

Alfalfa camped a lot as a hunting guide. Franks and beans are a good camping dish— and about all Alfalfa could afford back home on his range.

Alfalfa's Franks and Beans

He'd heat a can of beans, and when he could afford it he'd add maple syrup or brown sugar and a little cooked bacon. Then he'd split the hot dog lengthwise and broil it. Eat together.

"I just acquired five thousand fish."

"Five thousand? If it can be told, where did you take on this fine bundle of lettuce?"

"I have nothing to hide. I collected the reward on my father."

"It is an advantage to have a successful father. Nobody ever wanted my old man for as much as five hundred."

GUYS AND DOLLS, 1955

Debbie Reynolds

Debbie Reynolds was a bundle of talent wrapped up in the cutest little package you ever did see. She broke into pictures at age sixteen and within four short years was a full-fledged movie star, holding her own opposite Gene Kelly in *Singin' in the Rain*. Debbie was dynamite. With so much talent in one area, it figures she'd be lacking in others. Her talent in picking men was strictly amateur.

Debbie isn't completely to blame for the first one, Eddie Fisher. The popular crooner had a lot of people fooled. When they married in 1955, fan magazines declared it to be the perfect union. They delighted at the arrival of kids Carrie and Todd. The Fishers were the perfect '50s family, the envy of the nation.

The trouble started when Eddie's best friend, producer Mike Todd, the brains behind the box-office phenomenon *Around the World in 80 Days,* fell for Elizabeth Taylor. Eddie and Debbie stood up for them at their wedding, a quiet affair.

Above: Debbie and Eddie Fisher in happier times.

The honeymoon, however, was extravagant even by Hollywood standards . . . around the world in four hundred days for the globetrotting Todds. For over a year, the couple were inseparable. Then Mike had to fly to New York, a cold forcing Elizabeth to stay behind.

Hours later, Elizabeth learned the plane had crashed. Mike was dead. Pushed to the edge by grief and a relentless public, the widow withdrew from view.

A few months later, good friends Debbie and Eddie brought Liz back to the social whirl. "Eddie makes Mike seem more alive," Liz told friends. The rumors started right away. Then Broadway columnist Earl Wilson broke a story that filled headlines for months to come. "Elizabeth Taylor and Eddie Fisher were dancing it up at the Harwyn this morning, Eddie having been Mike Todd's close friend and now sort of an escort service for Liz." Seemed innocent, but between the lines it was a bombshell.

> *"She had a face like a Sunday school picnic. Do you have any idea what kind of face that is?"*
> MURDER, MY SWEET, 1944

The spotlight turned to Debbie in Beverly Hills. The press gathered at the Fisher home as if war were about to be declared. Cool and calm, Debbie put the kibosh on the gossip, assuring her fans that Eddie was just being a good pal. Nothing more. "My marriage is perfect." She rushed to the airport to meet him, the press in tow to capture the happy reunion. The plane came in . . . but Fisher wasn't on it. Ouch.

Debbie's next move had to be just right and she tied a ribbon on it, appearing in front of her house not as a glamorpuss, but in pigtails with diaper pins on her blouse. She looked like everybody's kid sister, bravely keeping the home fires burning while her husband ran around with some hussy. She still loved him, she told the press, but she might have to consult her attorney.

Overnight, Elizabeth Taylor became a scarlet woman and Fisher a cad. When he

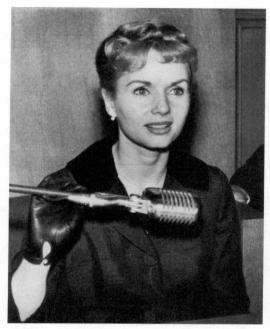

Debbie told the judge, "My husband has become interested in another woman"—like he might not have heard (February 1959).

Liz shows off her ring (June 1959).

opened in Vegas, she sat ringside. Protesters marched in front of the hotel. The sponsor of Fisher's TV show pulled out as newspapers and pulpits denounced his disgraceful behavior. Debbie was stoic and dignified . . . and kept her mouth shut. Her popularity soared.

Debbie and Eddie divorced in 1959. Liz and Eddie wed the same year. Elizabeth was offered the lead in *Cleopatra* and became the first actor to receive a million dollars for a film. The shoot was in London and the Fishers were grateful for an excuse to leave the country. Production delays were endless and Elizabeth collapsed under the stress. She contracted double pneumonia, with her temperature soaring to 108°. Some of the London papers even reported she had died. Miraculously, she recovered. Now the former home wrecker was a national heroine. Hollywood forgave her too. She won the Oscar for a mediocre film in which she played a call girl, *Butterfield 8.* Fellow nominee Shirley MacLaine later said she "lost the Oscar to a tracheotomy."

In the public's eye, all debts were settled. Taylor survived a brush with death and regained the favor of those who once condemned her. She met Richard Burton while shooting *Cleopatra* and Fisher was soon ancient history. To this day, the public is still trying to figure out what either woman ever saw in him. And Debbie? A real Hollywood survivor, she made her husband's affair work to her advantage, gaining tremendous public sympathy by doing what she'd planned to do anyway: divorce the rat.

As a newly single mom, Debbie learned to feed her kids on a budget.

Tacos

1	small onion, chopped
1	pound ground sirloin
1	tablespoon chili powder
	Salt and pepper to taste
1	tablespoon flour
½	can tomato sauce
12	taco shells or tortillas
½	pound grated cheese
	Chopped tomatoes
	Olives
	Lettuce

In a skillet brown the onion, and add the ground beef. Brown until almost completely done. Add the chili powder, salt, pepper, flour, and tomato sauce.

Fill the taco shells or put a small amount of meat in the middle of each tortilla, fold, and fry in a small amount of oil until crisp. Fill the shells with grated cheese, chopped tomato, olives, and lettuce—or anything else that suits your taste.

Montgomery Clift

Montgomery Clift was truly one of the most gifted actors of his generation, gifted in so many ways: talent, looks, charm, education, wit, and he had it by the armload—everything, it seems, but inner strength. There was a flaw deep in his core. Maybe he didn't believe in anything. How could he? His life was based on a lie. That lie and a terrible accident destroyed him.

An actor from age twelve, on Broadway at fourteen, Clift astonished audiences with his depth and sensitivity. He gave Hollywood the air until 1946. Then he gave them the double whammy: an Oscar nomination his first time out for *The Search* and a hotter-than-hot sensation as John Wayne's rebellious son in *Red River*. Clift, twenty-six, was something new: beautiful, vulnerable, intense, driven—that rare combination of genius and gorgeous. He exuded star quality. Men and women loved him. In *A Place in the Sun,* he steamed up the screen opposite nineteen-year-old and luscious Elizabeth Taylor.

Clift, thirty-one, became Hollywood's hottest male star and earned a second Oscar nomination. A third Oscar nomination followed for *From Here to Eternity*. He and Taylor began a lifelong friendship. Young Liz wished it could be more. Monty did too, but he couldn't; it was part of what ate at him.

See, in Hollywood, nothing is as it seems. Celebrities walk a thin line between their public and private lives. In Monty's case, it was particularly difficult. He adored women, but he was attracted to men. He fought his homosexuality, which meant there was always a battle going on within, always a bit of sadness. The pressure builds. A cocktail or a pill can remove that sadness, relieve that pressure. But you have to find a balance, know your limit. It wasn't easy. And Monty crashed big-time.

In May 1957, Monty and Elizabeth Taylor reteamed for the Civil War drama *Raintree County*. One night during the shoot, Monty attended an informal party at Liz and Michael Wilding's. Rock Hudson was there with his wife, along with Kevin McCarthy.

"What's the matter? Don't you like your steak medium?"

"When I bite a steak, I like it to bite back at me."

THE GLASS KEY, 1942

After the party broke up, Kevin followed Monty down the dark, winding canyon road toward Sunset Boulevard. Monty wasn't much of a driver to begin with, and that night, two other things worked against him: booze and pills. He lost control of his car and slammed into a telephone pole. His nose and jaw were broken, his sinus cavity smashed, and the cuts were to the bone. His face, his beautiful face, was crushed and shattered and ripped away. McCarthy ran for help. By the time Elizabeth got there, Monty's head had swollen to double its size. She cradled it and saved his life by reaching down his throat for his two front teeth; he was choking on them.

His face would never be the same. Neither would his mind or spirit. Bright, charming, the most beautiful man in Hollywood—all gone in an instant. The left side of his face was permanently paralyzed and all the muscles in his upper lip were severed. He had to learn new acting techniques to make up for it. Old friends didn't recognize him. It wasn't a bad face, but it was such a different face. Some say this began "the longest suicide in Hollywood," a downward spiral of booze and drugs. Nine months later, Clift finished *Raintree County,* a mediocre film at best, but huge at the box office. Everybody wanted to pick out the "before and after" Monty.

Monty before the accident . . .   . . . and after.

Clift retreated deep within himself, a loner. He looked shell-shocked. Most of the time, he stayed numb from his special concoction of crushed-up pills, vodka, and grapefruit juice in a thermos he drank from all day long. Odd behavior was reported on the set and in public. Guests at the Chateau Marmont hotel in Hollywood complained of his drunken ranting delivered in the nude from his balcony. Utterly tortured, Clift's drinking and drug problems began to affect his work and his bankability.

Liz asked for him for *Suddenly, Last Summer* in 1959. *Judgment at Nuremberg* in '61 gave him another plum role as an unbalanced victim of Nazi atrocities. His disturbing look worked for the role, and flashes of brilliance brought a fourth and final Academy Award nomination. Clift and costar Judy Garland bonded deeply during the filming, two troubled souls stuffing down the pain with pills and liquor. Monty took third billing to Clark Gable and Marilyn Monroe for the chance to work on John Huston's troubled production of *The Misfits* that same year. He and Marilyn were buddies from the Actors Studio, and they leaned on each other heavily during the grueling shoot. They commiserated, but didn't raise each other up. "He's the only person I know who's in worse shape than I am," Marilyn commented. Monty drank excessively and, during the entire production, spoke only to Marilyn and his makeup man. His self-control slipped away. His grace and charm evaporated. This once handsome, erudite man became intolerable. Friends stopped calling. Maybe he didn't notice. Maybe he was too gone to care. He grew weaker, developed terrible cataracts, couldn't remember lines; a wild, frightened look filled his eyes. The death of the spirit and the soul was complete. He had only to wait for the physical death. It wouldn't be long now.

Monty bought a four-story brownstone in Manhattan on East Sixty-first Street. Too weak or too unsteady to walk, he was carried from room to room by his "personal secretary"—on second thought, make that "nurse"—Lorenzo James. On Monday, July 22, 1966, Monty spent the day closed off in his bedroom. He barely spoke, except to ask Lorenzo for a goose liver sandwich. Much later, around 1:00 a.m., Lorenzo said good night. The Misfits was on TV; did Monty want to watch? "Absolutely not!" he replied, possibly his last words. He died during the night. Lorenzo found him lying faceup in bed, fists clenched, wearing only glasses. He was forty-five years old. The anguish was over. The end had finally come.

Monty's Goose Liver Sandwich

Sauté the goose liver in goose fat until soft. Cool. Place the liver in a bowl with three hard-boiled eggs, salt and pepper, paprika, and chopped onion. Blend until smooth but not oily. Spread on thin slices of toast.

Inger Stevens

What a package Inger Stevens came in: blonde, gorgeous, and every inch Swedish. But that doll was born behind the eight ball: broken home, no motherly influence, cold S.O.B. of a father, a lot of love affairs that went nowhere, and a lot of lonely nights. Despite a great career, the poor thing was so depressed, she killed herself—except that just doesn't add up. I'll give it to you straight and let you decide.

In 1953, at eighteen, Inger left her unhappy childhood behind and got a job dancing in New York's Latin Quarter at night. During the day, she pounded the pavement for acting work. With her looks—and talent besides—she got places pretty fast: commercials, then television plays, and finally, in 1956, Broadway.

Inger married her agent, an older man who showed her little affection—big surprise, a carbon copy of her dad. It lasted six months. She followed it with a string of older, even colder men: James Mason, Bing Crosby, a very married Anthony Quinn, and an also mar-

Dishing with Bing—who dumped her soon after.

ried Harry Belafonte. That's the one that really broke her heart. When it hit the skids, Inger, then twenty-three, attempted suicide. The papers reported the fling was with Bing, and that after he gave her the air for Kathy, she took a long swig on a bottle of cleaning fluid and went blind for two weeks. Stevens biographer William T. Patterson says that's a bunch of malarkey. "It was over Belafonte. She took pills and was in a coma for a few days. When she came out of it, she told friends it was the stupidest thing she ever did." Inger never tried anything like that again, but the press is like an elephant; they never forget. Inger was branded as frail, tragic, always looking for love, but never finding it. "The opposite was true," Patterson insists.

It's just that the love Inger found was strictly hush-hush during the volatile early days of the civil rights movement. By then, Inger was the very popular star of the top ten TV series *The Farmer's Daughter*. Her fans in the heartland and the Deep South would have dropped their socks to know the peaches-and-cream beauty was married to a black man. Gossip mavens Hedda Hopper and Louella Parsons had the goods on her. It would have been huge, a story that most likely would've ended her career, the times being what they were. Those evil broads must've liked Inger, because they never blew the whistle.

Inger's husband didn't let marriage get in the way of his love life. He was never faithful. Inger found comfort in the arms of her leading men. She compared making movies to being on a cruise—she and her costar were in love while the ship sailed; back in port, it was all over. After *Five Card Stud* wrapped in 1968, Inger continued to sleep with Rat Packer Dean Martin. Patterson says they had fun, but Martin was never sober. It ended when Dean asked her to bed his wife, Jeannie, while he looked on. Inger shared her reaction with pal Tom Mankiewicz, "Why is it I always pick pricks?"

In 1970, after nine years with her unfaithful husband, Inger wanted a divorce. She left her hubby in their small Malibu digs while she moved into their home in the Hollywood Hills—and into a romance with her costar, newcomer Burt Reynolds. Life looked rosy: She was set to star in a new TV series, got a new wardrobe, new beau, new lifestyle, whole new chapter. Sound depressed to you? Yeah, me neither.

April 29, 1970—Burt came over for dinner. Inger roasted lamb, poured a little champagne, but they argued and the manly Reynolds punched her on the jaw and left. It wasn't the first time some creep had thrown a punch at her. She put a bandage on her chin, sloughed off the incident, and sat down with the white phone. (There were two phones in the living room: black for her husband and white for everybody else; she thought it was funny.) She called a friend, her former partner in an antiques business. He'd found some antique furniture for her with a big cash discount. She called to tell him she'd gathered the $20,000 cash. They decided on a time for him to come get it the next day. Then she called her former assistant and best friend, Chris. She told her about Burt, invited her over to chat, play cards. Chris couldn't, so Inger said

Inger was making big changes when she suddenly died. Though her death was ruled a suicide, signs now point to murder.

she was going to take a sleeping pill and go to bed. "Talk to you tomorrow." That was at 11:00 P.M.

Lola, a friend, arrived the next morning. She was the first to find Inger's lifeless body, clad in a worn nightie, on the kitchen floor. Her arms were bruised, the bandage still on her chin. The coroner placed the time of death at around 6:00 A.M. There was a half-empty bottle of asthma medicine on the counter. Inger didn't have asthma. Neither did Lola or any of Inger's friends. Oh, and the twenty grand? That was gone.

"Reds"—Seconals—were scattered across the bedroom floor. Patterson says Inger occasionally took a sleeping pill, but when she did, it was a "rainbow," Tuinal. She didn't have a prescription for Seconal, and no bottle was ever found. "She was loaded with pills—twenty-five to fifty reds," says Patterson, "washed down with booze. She had no history of mixing pills and alcohol." Is that where the bruises on her arms came from? Someone forced her to take them?

One of the phones in the living room was gone; no one seems to remember which one. Her ex claimed he was at the beach, that he'd tried to call but the line was disconnected. The carpet in the bedroom was pushed back in an attempt to hide pictures of Burt. Seems Inger planned to sleep alone—the old nightie—and she got a surprise visitor, someone who might lose their temper seeing pictures of another man.

Folks, if an actress plans to kill herself, she sets the stage. That includes her best P.J.'s, not some ratty, everyday thing. Put the rest of the pieces together: new series, new clothes, new boyfriend, new furniture, plans for tomorrow, and oh yeah, she was fixing a sandwich. On the kitchen counter were all the makings for one of her favorites: a bacon, lettuce, and tomato sandwich with avocado. Who stops in the middle of a BLT to kill herself? "Let's see, a little more tomato, another bacon strip . . . oh, the hell with it, get the pills and liquor."

Though friends insisted she was clearly in high spirits, the press dug out that old suicide attempt as proof she was suicidal. Of all people, they interviewed her father, who said she was always unhappy. Tony Quinn acted like a big blowhard, talking to anyone who'd listen about poor Inger. Patterson laughs, "She couldn't stand him." A psychological autopsy was mournfully incomplete. Official conclusion: suicide. But I believe Inger Stevens has not had her just deserts. Stick around.

Scandinavians love sandwiches. Inger made a mean Club and a great tuna melt and she adored steak tartare on crackers, but her all-time fave, the midnight snack she was making when death interrupted, was this one:

The Inger Stevens BLT with Avocado

2	slices of bread
	Mayo or mustard
	Iceberg lettuce
1	tomato
3	slices of bacon
1	avocado

Lightly spread your choice of bread with mayonnaise or mustard (optional). Lay crisp, dry sheets of lettuce on one piece of bread. Slice the tomato to desired thickness and lay the rounds on top of the lettuce. Cook three pieces of bacon, drain, and place across the tomato slices. Halve the avocado, cut into slices, and place on top. Add the second piece of bread. Holding the sandwich firmly, cut diagonally through it with a sharp knife.

Cass Elliot

At 5'5" and 238 pounds, Cass Elliot was a big woman. Get it out of the way now. She sang like an angel, had a groovy sense of humor and a compassionate nature, but all anybody ever talked about was how fat she was. It tortured her. She tried every diet that came down the pike. The loss was never permanent, but she never stopped trying. Poor Cass, heart of gold, remained a magnet for all the ugly, fat girl jokes. Even the last newspaper headline of her life announced her arrival in London for a "heavy date." Ridicule followed her everywhere . . . even in death. Urban legend has her choking to death on a ham sandwich. That went around the world faster than Richard Gere and the gerbil. Here's the straight scoop: It never happened.

Ellen Cohen changed her name to Cass Elliot and moved to New York to sing. Cass was drawn to the smoky coffeehouses and bars of Greenwich Village where beatniks and folksingers were giving way to the Age of Aquarius. She waited tables, bounced from group to group, made a few records, and eventually joined the Mugwumps with Denny Doherty. Around '63, Denny joined John and Michelle Phillips in the New Journeymen. Cass wanted in, but they said no: Her size was a turnoff, and her voice was too low to blend with Michelle's. Funny how some people push their destiny away. Cass ran straight toward it, following them to the Virgin Islands. They sang as a foursome there in exchange for a place to crash. The trio had finally brought her into the circle. Then the magic began.

The comments never stopped. Two weeks before she died, London papers announced Cass's arrival for "a heavy date" at the Palladium, noting that "despite reports of strict dieting, she's still a substantial figure."

As The Mamas and the Papas, they soon scored a recording contract in L.A. John was the leader, Michelle the beauty, Denny the harmony, and Mama Cass, well, she was pure charisma and powerful voice. The quartet topped the charts with classics like "Go Where You Wanna Go," "California Dreamin'," and "Monday Monday."

Cass charmed fans with her big smile and gentle spirit, but behind the smile were tears. Desperately unhappy about her size, she tried pills and crazy crash diets. When she did drop weight, she'd balloon up again. It was a losing battle, just like her love life. She told Michelle that she carried a torch for Denny, but he wasn't interested. Cass had a daughter in '67, but she wouldn't reveal who the father was. She never married.

By 1968, Michelle and her husband, John, had problems too. Suddenly Denny looked good to her. Their life as a group was a soap opera. Michelle and Denny betrayed both John and Cass with a brief, passionate fling. Michelle and John broke up. Then the group broke up. But Cass hung in there. On her own in the early '70s she had big solo hits like: "It's Gettin' Better" and "Make Your Own Kind of Music." She did talk shows, concerts, even had a movie role. At thirty-two, life was good. In July 1974, her career going gangbusters, Cass was in London, staying in singer Harry Nilsson's flat. Next thing you know, she's dead.

When you check out like that, expect wild rumors, like she OD'd on heroin. Another said she was carrying John Lennon's baby. Her physician told the press she "probably choked to death on a sandwich." That wasn't his medical opinion, just his pathetic personal thoughts about a fat girl. With doctors like that, who needs enemies? By the next week, reports listed a "ham sandwich" as the fatal meal. Ham, pig . . . a cruel side dish added to a nonexistent last supper. People laughed, never doubting that Big Mama choked to death, eating in bed.

A week later the facts got in the way of the laughter. The autopsy revealed no traces of food blocking the trachea. No bread, no ham, no mayo. Cass died from a heart attack, the result of long-term obesity and crash diets. And now there's a new twist. After more than two decades of study, experts believe her heart attack was induced by sleep apnea, a common disorder in the obese. The back of the mouth slips down onto the tongue, causing suffocation and, often, a heart attack. But that's not entertainment. The ham sandwich story lived on for years, but it's over now. The fat lady has sung on that one, honey.

The Mamas and the Papas found musical and spiritual harmony in the Virgin Islands. Back home in L.A., they often cooked their favorite dish from the Islands. They could not remember the name of the woman who gave them the recipe, so they used their own cook's name, Esperanza. She made it for them often and well. This is a good recipe to make ahead, then heat up just before serving time. Cass loved it with scrambled eggs.

Chili Esperanza

4 servings

½	pound butter
2	large Bermuda onions, sliced
2	green peppers, sliced
1½	pounds ground beef
	Dash of garlic, salt, pepper, cayenne
2	tablespoons chili powder (less if you don't like it HOT)
1	large can red kidney beans, drained

In a large skillet melt the butter. Cover the bottom of the skillet with the sliced onions and peppers. Cook slowly, until the onions are golden and transparent and the peppers are soft. Add the meat, and spread it around so that it covers the onions and peppers. Let it brown, but don't overcook it. As soon as all the pink disappears from the meat and it is brown, add the spices and the kidney beans. Mix it all up; cover and simmer for 30 minutes, stirring occasionally.

Cocktails

William Desmond Taylor 53

Thelma Todd 61

Charles Farrell..71

Errol Flynn 77

Dorothy Kilgallen 81

"Come on. Let's get something to eat. I'm thirsty."
AFTER THE THIN MAN, 1936

"One martini is alright, two is too many, three is not enough."
JAMES THURBER

"I would sell my grandmother for a drink—and you know how I love my grandmother."
THE PHILADELPHIA STORY, 1940

William Desmond Taylor

The Taylor case—there's nothing else like it in all of Hollywood history. On a chilly February morning in 1922, William Desmond Taylor, at forty-five one of Paramount's leading directors, was found shot to death in his bungalow apartment. The number of stars caught up in the case alone makes it a standout; but startling revelations about their private lives and Taylor's quickly made the murder secondary to the resulting scandals.

William Desmond Taylor was elegant, worldly, sophisticated. Hollywood was pretty wild in '22, and that made the "Gentleman Director" something of a phenomenon. He was well-liked all around. Women were drawn to him, especially younger women, who found his maturity calming. Mary Pickford called him the most patient man she ever knew. His peers voted him president of the Screen Actors Guild, and he was highly regarded as a director. Bill Taylor shot? Impossible.

They say Taylor was in love with Mabel Normand, the silent screen's queen of com-

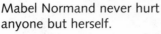
Mabel Normand never hurt
anyone but herself.

edy. He'd proposed several times but Mabel just
couldn't commit. She drifted in and out of his
life and hadn't even seen him for two months till the night he was
shot. She came by to borrow some books. Henry Peavey, Taylor's servant, greeted her
coldly. He'd seen Taylor crying over her photograph. He served them drinks, then left for
the evening. At 7:45, Mabel rose to go. Taylor left his front door ajar and escorted Mabel
to her car. That's when police think someone slipped inside. They found cigarettes crushed
out in the alleyway between Taylor's and his neighbors, the MacLeans. The MacLeans'
maid heard someone out there around 7:30.

About 8:00, Faith McLean heard a gunshot. She looked out just in time to see a man
leaving Taylor's bungalow. He wore a long coat, collar up, a muffler, and a hat. When he
spotted Faith, he leaned back into Taylor's doorway as if to say good night, cool as anything. Then he walked to the trolley and disappeared. Taylor's lights stayed on all night,
but no one thought anything about it until they heard Peavey screaming the next morning that Mr. Taylor was dead.

The phone calls started right away, but not to the police. This was no time for the
cops. Studio executives raced to Taylor's to remove anything that might tarnish his reputation . . . and theirs by association. When the cops finally got there, people were burning papers in the fireplace and removing cases of illegal booze. Mabel Normand was
scouring the place for her love notes and nineteen-year-old Mary Miles Minter was hysterical outside. She should have been. Police found dainty underthings with MMM
embroidered on them in Taylor's bedroom.

Right away, the cops suspected his former valet, Edward Sands. While Taylor was in Europe in 1921, Sands grabbed everything he could, forging checks and stealing clothes, jewelry, even the car. By the time Taylor returned and filed charges, Sands was long gone. A month before Taylor was murdered, he received a pawn ticket for one of the stolen items. The ticket was signed Deane Tanner. Police wanted to know who that was.

Go figure . . . it was Taylor.

William Desmond Taylor was really William Cunningham Deane Tanner. No gentleman, he'd deserted a wife and child in New York in 1908, changed his name, waltzed into Los Angeles, and gotten work as an actor. His wife saw him on-screen, searched him out, and asked for money for their daughter. Taylor had sent a monthly check since then. Friends, including Normand, were more than a little surprised.

By 1914, Taylor was making a name for himself as a director, keeping his past under tight wraps. But Sands found out. How? Wait'll you hear this one: Taylor had a brother, Dennis, who disappeared from New York the same way as Taylor four years later. Maybe Sands was really Dennis, who was blackmailing his famous brother. The cops figured when Taylor refused to give Sands/Dennis what he wanted, he was shot. There was a nationwide search, but they never found him. Meanwhile, Faith MacLean had seen Sands many times and was positive the figure she saw leaving Taylor's was not Sands.

Police dismissed Mabel Normand as a suspect, but in the process they uncovered a darker side. She traveled with the fast crowd, and the fast crowd used drugs. She was a "hophead," a coke addict. Out of concern for her, Taylor had confronted several dealers, trying to drive them out. Could these dealers have hired a professional killer to take him out? Cops rounded up the underbelly of L.A., but they couldn't come up with a shred of evidence. Instead they looked in a different direction: toward Mary Miles Minter's nightie.

> "I shouldn't oughta be talkin' to ya, but when I like a guy and he buys me a drink, the ceiling's the limit."
>
> MURDER MY SWEET, 1944

Mary Miles Minter and her monstrous mother, Charlotte Shelby.

Minter, all long blonde curls and virginal innocence, was a star with a contract at Paramount worth over a million dollars. Dad wasn't in the picture and Mom was a nightmare. Ruthless and manipulative, Charlotte Shelby controlled her daughter and all the money she made. Taylor tried to get Mary to break with her mother, encouraged her to live on her own. Mary took his concern for love. She fell hard for him. Taylor may or may not have returned those feelings. But Shelby was not about to let her daughter marry, leave the house, and keep her own money. She publicly threatened to shoot Taylor if he ever went near Mary.

The killer held a .38-caliber Smith and Wesson revolver just an inch or two from Taylor's left side. The holes in his jacket and his vest match only if his arm was raised. Did someone yell, "Hands up"? Was he embracing someone? Charlotte could never have gotten that close. Did Mary rush there to save him only to accidentally kill him? Did she and Charlotte wrestle for the gun? Three blonde hairs were found on his jacket. Cops thought it matched Mary's. Rumor spread that maybe it was Charlotte, dressed as a man,

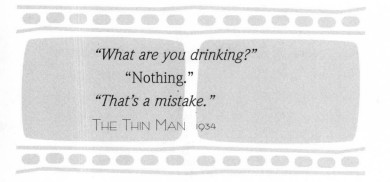

"What are you drinking?"
"Nothing."
"That's a mistake."
THE THIN MAN 1934

that Faith MacLean had seen at Taylor's door. She told police that at the time of the murder she was at her home with a friend, bit player Carl Stockdale, and that was that. She was never questioned further and promptly left for three months in Europe. Stockdale received a check from Shelby for $200 a month for the rest of his life.

When her fans found out that Mary Miles Minter had been throwing herself at a man more than twice her age, they gave her the air. Paramount had been losing money on Mary's films before the scandal. Some folks wondered if the studio hadn't planted her underclothes at Taylor's to void their contract. However they got there, they did the trick. Charlotte's golden goose was dead.

There was a star-studded coroner's inquest, but Taylor's murder was never solved. The weapon was never found. Bullets identical to the one that killed Taylor were found in Shelby's house fifteen years after the murder. There's evidence to support the theory that Shelby paid off three generations of district attorneys to stay out of jail. The last one killed himself with a .38 Smith and Wesson. When she ran out of money in 1957—make that ran out of Mary's money—she had herself legally declared dead. She lived with Mary and never again ventured out.

Cut to 1963. Ray Long answered the cries of an elderly neighbor who collapsed in her home. He called for an ambulance and while they waited, she made a confession. "I killed

"Hollywood is wonderful. Anyone who doesn't like it is either crazy or sober."
RAYMOND CHANDLER

William Desmond Taylor." She died an hour later. Long did not know who Taylor or his neighbor were, but he spent the next five years finding out.

Margaret Gibson, sixteen, met Taylor when he was thirty-three and working theaters in Denver around 1910. The following year, in Hollywood, they worked together on at least four films. By 1918, Gibson, an aging ingenue, tried to put a spin on her career with a new name, Patricia Palmer. It worked, for a while. In early '22, she got work in a serial Western shooting on the Paramount lot. She'd have seen Taylor, successful, respected, young girls vying for his attention. Had they been an item not so long ago? Had he patted her shoulder, told her to come round? Could the blonde hairs on his coat have been

Hope that thermos is full of Orange Blossoms.
Bottoms up!

hers? Palmer retired in '29, then spent three quiet decades in the Hollywood Hills holding on to her little secret. Did the forgotten actress make a last grab for a dubious place in film history? Or was she some addled old lady lost in the past? We will never have the answer.

In 1967, director King Vidor thought all this would make a great movie and decided to do a little investigating into the murder of his old friend Bill Taylor. He visited Mary, then sixty-five, in Santa Monica. Huge and grotesque, she became frantic at the mention of Taylor and sobbed convulsively at every mention of her mother. Vidor wasn't sure if he'd caught a glimpse of Charlotte in the upstairs window. Dark curtains, dust everywhere, Mary reading poetry. It was surreal. He couldn't get out of there fast enough. Before he did, Mary said something that chilled him to the bone. "My mother killed everything I ever loved."

Henry Peavey served Mabel and Mr. Taylor the most popular cocktail of the day, even with Prohibition in full swing. It's the last thing that touched his lips.

Orange Blossoms

1½ ounces gin
¼ teaspoon sugar
Juice of half an orange

Shake well with cracked ice and strain into a martini glass.

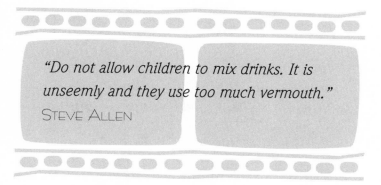

"Do not allow children to mix drinks. It is unseemly and they use too much vermouth."
STEVE ALLEN

"I gave her a drink. She was a gal who'd take a drink if she had to knock ya down to get the bottle."

MURDER, MY SWEET, 1944

"I'd like to ask you to stay and have a drink, but I'm afraid you might accept."

THE FEMALE ON THE BEACH, 1955

"I was in love with a beautiful blonde once, dear. She drove me to drink. That's the one thing I'm indebted to her for."

NEVER GIVE A SUCKER AN EVEN BREAK, 1941

"You can't drown yourself in drink. I've tried, you float."

JOHN BARRYMORE

Thelma Todd

Most Sincerely,
Thelma
Todd

There was a reason they called her Hot Toddy. Thelma Todd was a real sweetheart. A former model, Thelma appeared in silent films in New York then headed for Hollywood, where flappers and their sheiks zoomed down the Sunset Strip in fast, open cars; where big money could be made quickly; and where a girl like Thelma could really go places. And sister, she tied a ribbon on it. But in 1935, Thelma hit a dead end; the luscious thirty-year-old was found dead in her garage. Exactly how she got there was a mystery for some sixty years. That's because people held back ingredients to this recipe for murder.

Toddy's beauty, wit, and impeccable timing made her the perfect foil for the comedy greats of the day, including Jimmy Durante, Laurel and Hardy, and the Marx Brothers. Fans loved her in two series of comedy shorts she starred in for Hal Roach—the first with gawky, scatterbrained sidekick ZaSu Pitts and the second with chubby, deadpan Patsy Kelly. At the box office, Hot Toddy was a hot ticket. No, Thelma's work was not her problem.

There was a weight problem. Thelma was packing on the pounds—booze'll do that—so she began popping diet pills. Then she'd get behind the wheel. The cops ticketed her repeatedly for speeding and driving under the influence. After she crashed into a palm tree near Hollywood Boulevard and suffered serious injuries, Roach forbade her to drive. Thelma hired people to drive for her, but they couldn't deliver Todd from the collision course she was on.

She lived with a married man, director Roland West, forty-eight, and had foolishly become business partners with him in a chic, oceanside restaurant that bore her name.

"The important thing is the rhythm. You always have rhythm in your shaking. Now a Manhattan you shake to a foxtrot, a Bronx to a 2-step time, a dry Martini you always shake to waltz time."
THE THIN MAN, 1934

West and Todd lived in apartments above the café while West's wife, Jewell Carmen, lived in West's cliffside villa, Castillo del Mar—"Castle by the Sea"—several hundred yards above the restaurant. West was possessive and controlling and now Thelma wanted out. She had affairs and pursued partying full-tilt down the fast lane.

At 10:30 A.M. on Monday, December 16, Thelma's maid, Mae Whitehead, began her morning ritual. She drove up the winding hills of the Pacific Palisades to the garages under Castillo del Mar. As usual, she would leave her car there and drive Miss Todd's chocolate brown Lincoln Phaeton to the entrance of the restaurant, the familiar signal that Thelma Todd's Sidewalk Café was open for business.

This morning, when she opened the garage door, Whitehead found Thelma slumped behind the wheel, still wearing evening clothes from Saturday night. "Wake up, honey," Mae whispered gently. But the Blond Venus was dead.

Robbery was not the motive. Thelma was wearing a full-length mink coat and $20,000 worth of jewelry. There were no signs of violence. Blood on her upper lip was consistent with carbon monoxide poisoning. LAPD noted the car's ignition was on; the battery dead. They considered suicide, but Thelma's mother screamed bloody murder.

Thelma dishes with her husband, agent Pat Di Cicco.

Her cries brought down a plague of reporters who generated controversy, conflicting reports and lurid accounts of Thelma's mysterious last hours.

Here's what we know for sure. At 8:00 P.M. on Saturday, December 14, Ernest Peters arrived in a limousine to deliver Thelma to a party in her honor given by Ida Lupino and her parents at the fashionable Café Trocadero. West told her to be home by 2:00. She told West to stuff it.

Toddy joined the party of fourteen waiting for her in the Troc's cocktail lounge. Thelma sparkled, in her usual high spirits—even after a small "incident" with Pat Di Cicco, her ex-husband, a hot-blooded man known for hitting first and asking questions later. Toddy had reserved a seat next to her for him, but Di Cicco dined and danced with actress Margaret Lindsay in another room. Thelma shrugged it off. "It means nothing," she said.

At 11:45, a hatcheck girl observed Thelma on the phone in the ladies' room. ". . . afterwards, she was upset. She said she was fine, but I could see she wasn't."

Almost everyone noticed Thelma's mood change, but Thelma stayed at the party until 3:15. Ernest Peters pulled up in front of her café just before 4:00 A.M. He later testified that Thelma declined his customary offer to escort her to her apartment door. It was cold and foggy. He watched her close her mink against the wind and start up the stairs. Then he drove away.

West later explained that he'd bolted the door from the inside when he retired at 2:30. When Thelma wasn't there Sunday morning, he assumed she'd gone to her

Thelma's seaside café.

mother's as was her custom. Nine people, including Jewell Carmen, swore they saw or spoke to Thelma well after the coroner's estimated time of death. Several said she was in the company of a "dark stranger." The last two were Christmas tree salesmen who told reporters they sold a tree to Ms. Todd and the stranger around 11:00 P.M. Sunday. The couple asked for the tree to be silvered and said they would return shortly. They never did. What's more, the salesmen said two tough guys came by the lot a few days later and told them to keep their mouths shut about who and what they saw. A waiter at the Trocadero received a kidnap threat. Supposedly, even Mae Whitehead was threatened.

The press reported Thelma had broken ribs, teeth knocked down her pretty throat, and strangulation-type bruises.

All this dirty work conveniently pointed a finger at the mob. Scuttlebutt was that Lucky Luciano, a close pal of Di Cicco's, wanted to operate gambling facilities above Thelma's café. Thelma said no; now reporters and gossip insinuated she had paid the

The death garage.

price. Police advanced the theory that, locked out, Thelma decided to sleep in her car. Intoxicated, fighting the wind and cold, she climbed the steep 271 stairs behind the café to the garage. Once there, she started the engine to keep warm and dozed off before being overcome by the fumes. Her death was a terrible accident. Case closed.

Cut to 1987. Authors Marvin Wolf and Katherine Mader did some investigating of their own and in their search, uncovered a very credible answer to a question that has haunted Hollywood: Who iced the Ice Cream Blonde?

Let's set the scene: Film, business, and civic leaders of Hollywood were already on edge in December of 1935. On the very day Thelma's body was found, director Busby Berkeley went on trial for three counts of murder. He killed three people driving drunk on the Pacific Coast Highway not far from Thelma's restaurant. The last thing Hollywood needed was another celebrity murder trial.

Joe Schenck, a Russian immigrant, got into show business launching his own operation with none other than Roland West in 1912. By 1935, Schenck was chairman of the board of 20th Century-Fox and one of California's wealthiest and most powerful men. His brother was head of Loew's and MGM, which made him the boss of Hal Roach, the man who'd made Thelma a star. Schenck adored Thelma and had a contract waiting for her if she ever left Roach.

> *"I'm not married. I have no designs on you. And one drink is all I care for."*
> THE WOMAN IN THE WINDOW, 1944

In 1987, Wolf and Mader interviewed Hal Roach, who, at age ninety, was alert and full of energy, with a remarkable memory. And he'd outlived all concerned, so he got straight to the point. The day after Thelma's body was discovered, he was visited by three L.A. County sheriff's detectives. They told him that, after intense questioning, West had confessed to killing Thelma.

"West was very possessive," he said. "He told her to be back at 2:00. She said she'd come and go as she pleased. They argued and Thelma left for the party." He added that when she was late, West locked her out to teach her a lesson.

When Thelma arrived home at 4:00 A.M., she knew there would be a scene, so she told Ernest Peters to go. There was an argument through the locked door and Thelma marched up to the garage. She was already in her car, engine running, by the time West got there. He shut the door and locked her in. "He wasn't thinking about carbon monoxide, just about teaching her who was boss. He left and went back to bed," Roach explained.

After sunrise, he went to let her out and discovered her body. "He didn't know what

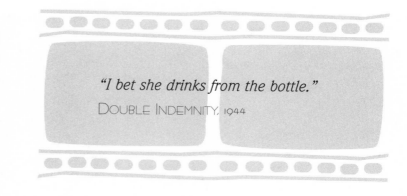

"I bet she drinks from the bottle."
Double Indemnity, 1944

to do," said Roach, "so he did nothing. He closed the door and went back to the café. All that day when people called for Thelma, he said he didn't know where she was. If he really hadn't known, he would have been calling all over trying to find her. That's the kind of man he was."

Wolf and Mader were shocked and amazed. Roach had not only named the killer, he had admitted his part in the cover-up. Why would Roach protect the man who killed one of his biggest stars? Implicating West would have exposed Thelma's affair with him, as well as a passel of her personal problems with resulting scandal and box-office losses for Roach. But there was more. For that, they'd have to dig deeper.

After days spent in stacks of dusty files, Wolf and Mader had their answer. The cover-up hinged on one man: Sheriff Eugene Biscailuz. In 1932, Biscailuz resigned from the California Highway Patrol to win his election. In his previous position, he was well acquainted with former highway commissioner Joe Schenck. Biscailuz was also a close friend of ZaSu Pitts, Thelma's nearest and dearest and a heavy contributor to Biscailuz's election campaign. And he knew Roland West as a fellow 32nd-degree Mason and lodge brother. Small world, isn't it?

Schenck had a real personal reason for wanting to keep West out of things. In 1935, Schenck used West in a tax fraud scheme. He was desperately afraid West might trade information about the scam in return for a reduced sentence. (Schenck would eventually be convicted of tax evasion in 1941.)

L.A.'s police department of 1935 was dirty. Justice was bought back then. Add to that, Biscailuz was personally connected with all the major players in the case. What's more, as sheriff, he had an institutional interest in L.A. County's most visible and most important

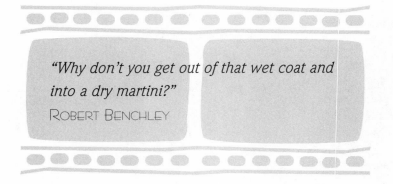

industry, the movies. And this mess could make the movies look very bad indeed. Biscailuz used his friendship with the deputy D.A., who helped present the Todd case to the grand jury, which—big surprise—returned no indictment. Schenck threw some money around, and "witnesses" pointed a distracting finger at the mob. According to a retired detective, only a handful of senior cops ever knew about West's confession.

So, poor Thelma Todd's death was left an accident. Roland West retreated from Hollywood, never made another film. On his deathbed in 1951, he confessed his guilt to actor Chester Morris, a close friend. Morris, before his suicide in 1972, repeated the confession to director Alex Gordon, who confirmed it to Wolf and Mader. In 1988, Don Gallery, ZaSu Pitts's adopted son, revealed that his mother had confided an almost identical version of Thelma's death to him.

And so ended the life of one of Hollywood's most beautiful and popular stars: no mob hit, no tragic suicide, no unexplained sightings, no bloody trail . . . only a paper one.

Thelma was served a five-course meal at the Trocadero, but the only thing in her stomach was peas and carrots. Could the poor thing actually have stuck to her diet on the last night of her life? And the veggies were probably loaded with butter anyway. But her blood alcohol level was way up there. Thelma loved her cocktails.

The Three Finger, A New Old Fashioned, and the Joya

Rudy Schafer's father was a bartender at Thelma's club. He told his son Thelma's personal tipple was a Three Finger: three fingers of Rye whiskey, probably Old Overholt, a top brand of the day, with ice.

In May of '35, Harrison Carrol noted for the evening Herald Examiner:

"At Thelma Todd's beach café, they serve you a variety of an Old Fashioned cocktail that tastes much better than it sounds. Instead of whiskey, use two parts gin and one of Jamaica rum. Add dashes of maraschino."

Two weeks later Carrol wrote about the opening of Joya Restaurant:

". . . a swank, small capacity room will open June 23 on the second floor of Thelma Todd's Sidewalk Cafe. It'll offer one cocktail, the Joya, that costs $2.50 a copy. Made of champagne, peaches, and a little grenadine and served in Pilsner glasses, Roland West invented it."

"Where's my brandy?"

"I finished it for your own good."

SPELLBOUND, 1945

"Some day you'll drown in a vat of whiskey!"

"Drown in a vat of whiskey. Death, where is thy sting?"

NEVER GIVE A SUCKER AN EVEN BREAK, 1941

Charles Farrell

My *Little Margie* was a summer replacement for *I Love Lucy*. As Vernon Albright, Charles Farrell was sophisticated, elegant, a swell dresser—and constantly hot and bothered by his daughter, Margie (Gale Storm): cute as lace pants, but a real nitwit. A lot of the show's fans were unaware this was a comeback for Farrell. Turns out there's a lot about Charlie Farrell nobody knew.

The smooth and dapper Farrell escaped a hellish childhood right out of a Dickens novel. His parents weren't much more than work camp commandants. They showed no love and worked him so hard he barely had time for school. But Charlie was a dutiful son; he didn't whine. He did the work, but deep in his gut he was miserable. He fantasized about Hollywood, about the good life he could have as a movie star. At twenty-two, in 1923, he hit the road with $18 in his pocket to make that dream come true.

Charlie struggled at odd jobs and extra work while sleeping on friends' floors. After three years, his big break arrived, but like everything in Hollywood, it came with a price. *Old Ironsides* made him a star, but a stunt explosion gone wrong killed a technician and injured members of the cast and crew. Charlie's ears blew out—permanent damage that would plague him the rest of his life while laying the foundation for whispered rumors.

Women didn't care if he could hear. They were crazy about him. Handsome, smooth, with both feet on the ground, Charlie Farrell was a guy a girl could really talk to. Not like, say, Ronald Colman or John Gilbert or even Barrymore; they were like your best china. Charlie was for every day. He and the sweet and wholesome Janet Gaynor created one of the silver screen's great romantic teams. "America's Favorite Lovebirds" were so convincing, the public believed they were an item offscreen as well, despite marriages to other people. They were the best of friends . . . and friends keep secrets. So said Hollywood's "Sewing Circle," a lesbian club of sorts that claimed Janet Gaynor as one of their own. And her marriage to costume designer Adrien? One of convenience, a beard. And the Circle didn't stop there. Charlie was handsome, but not exactly what you'd call virile . . . hmmm. Gaynor and Farrell were thought to be "the first known 'twilight tandem.'"

Anthony Slide, renowned film historian and a gay man, figures it this way: "Most gossip, of course, comes second- or third-hand, and identification of many performers as gay or lesbian is more wishful thinking on the part of the gay community than fact. Because early talkies leading man Charles Farrell has a high-pitched voice and a slightly effeminate mannerism, he is assumed to be gay. Any marriage Farrell entered into would have been one of convenience, with the implication that his wife, actress Virginia Valli, was a lesbian. Yet there is no evidence to support such a contention."

Charlie's occasional high notes may go back to that explosion. He couldn't adjust what he couldn't hear. But the public's fondness for Charlie survived sound as well as his marriage to pretty Virginia Valli. She married Charlie in 1931 and, after more than sixty films, retired.

In 1933, Charlie expanded his interest. Palm Springs was a favorite getaway for the Hollywood crowd. Charlie loved it there and bought several acres of desert in Palm Springs with fellow actor Ralph Bellamy. The Ralph Bellamy and Charles Farrell Racquet Club consisted of two tennis courts and a dressing room. And the movie colony loved it. As the word spread, so did the club: more courts, a hotel, a restaurant, and, of course, a

Charlie dishes
with his Mrs.—
and Darryl
Zanuck's, too.

Charlie and Virginia in 1931:
his bride or his beard?

bar Charlie called the Bamboo Lounge. In the late '30s, Bellamy sold out to Charlie. Virginia took over as manager and, together, the Farrells made millions.

The Racquet Club of Palm Springs became one of the premier desert hideaways. Charlie and Virginia hosted Hollywood's elite: Marilyn Monroe, Frank Sinatra, Clark Gable, Spencer Tracy, Ginger Rogers, and Cary Grant all came to play tennis, to relax, and to dine at the famous Bamboo Lounge. And for those who "relaxed" a little too hard, Charlie invented a hangover cure he called the Folding Farrell . . . better known today as the Bloody Mary. Charles Farrell was in his element—the old guard of filmland mixing with the new. And what revenue he brought to the little desert town. Palm Springs residents showed their gratitude by electing him mayor. He served for seven years, then, unexpectedly, made a spectacular Hollywood comeback.

Producer Hal Roach Jr. was a regular at the Club. While vacationing there, he offered Farrell the role in *My Little Margie.* Without benefit of a pilot and with only three weeks of rehearsal, he and Gale Storm created a small-screen dream team. The show ran three seasons, and for Charlie they were the happiest years of his life. In 1959, he and Virginia sold the Club for a reported $1.2 million. They traveled the world until her death in 1968. Charlie died in 1990, at age eighty-nine.

"Can't you get to sleep?"
"No."
"Maybe if you took a drink, it would help you."
"No, thank you."
"Maybe it would help if I took it."
THE THIN MAN, 1934

So was he or wasn't he? Rumors of homosexuality have followed Charlie Farrell to the grave. I figure it this way: Who cares? Farrell was handed lemons and made lemonade—barrels of it. When he left his cold, cruel home for Hollywood, all he really wanted was acceptance and love. He ended his days rolling in it. Man, that's slick. What a fairy tale. Here's lookin' at you, kid.

The Folding Farrell

	Dash of Lemon juice
	Worcestershire sauce
2	to 3 drops Tabasco sauce
	Pepper, salt, and celery salt
1¼	ounces vodka
	Tomato juice
	Celery stick
	Lime wedge

Fill a tall glass with ice and add the lemon juice, Worcestershire sauce, Tabasco sauce, and spices, then add the vodka. Fill with tomato juice and stir. Garnish with a celery stick and a lime wedge.

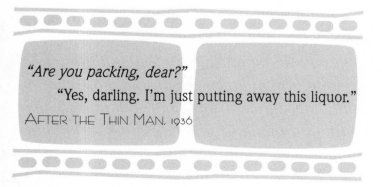

"Are you packing, dear?"

"Yes, darling. I'm just putting away this liquor."

AFTER THE THIN MAN, 1936

THE BEACHCOMBER CAFE   FAMOUS NIGHT SPOT   HOLLYWOOD, CAL. 49

Don the Beachcomber's reminded
Errol Flynn of the islands.

"You drinking that stuff this early?"
   "Listen, darling, when you drink as much
   as I do, you gotta start early."

CRY DANGER, 1951

Errol Flynn

Jack Warner, the boss of Warner Brothers Studios, described his star Errol Flynn as "all the heroes in one magnificent, sexy, animal package." Translation: Nobody in Hollywood got laid more than Errol Flynn. He arrived in 1935, by way of Tasmania. Tall, athletic, handsome, his first screen role was . . . a corpse—not a complicated part, unless you're Errol Flynn. He thought it was so funny, "the corpse" shook with laughter under the sheet. "Some people claim it was my best role," he later wrote.

Flynn did alright. In a short time, he had no rival on the screen as a romantic hero. He was big box office in films like *Captain Blood, Charge of the Light Brigade, Robin Hood.* Dashing and full of the devil, he thrilled audiences performing feats of daring. Men wanted to be like him, and women wanted to be with him. It's a safe bet his personal life was a rousing success. At twenty-six, he enthusiastically joined in the Hollywood nightlife. His nightclub brawls and amorous escapades entertained his fans in the gossip columns. Witty, debonair, and positively magnetic, Errol behaved like a mischievous boy, but most people found it impossible to dislike him. Errol Flynn, they said, could charm the birds out of the trees. But in 1942 the fun and games turned serious. Flynn was charged with the statutory rape of a seventeen-year-old girl.

"ROBIN HOOD CHARGED WITH RAPE." Most places, the headline was met with a wink and a nudge, but Flynn felt the sting of shame. The Grand Jury acquitted him pronto of the trumped-up charge; but that wasn't the end of it. The boys from Chicago were looking to get to Jack Warner. They'd extorted money from the other studios, but Warner couldn't be shaken. After Flynn's acquittal, they demanded ten grand or Warner's biggest star "won't know what hit him." Warner refused. That's when the district attorney suddenly overrode the grand jury's decision and prepared to prosecute Flynn. And they doubled the stakes: another teenager, another charge of statutory rape.

Warner didn't waste any time. He hired the attorney everybody called when they had a star in trouble; he got the best, Jerry Geisler. Dr. Mason Rose, an associate of the late, great Geisler and a personal friend of Flynn, confided what went on undercover. "Geisler had to maintain a 'no knowledge' policy or face charges of solicitation; so I handled the offers that came through the girls' attorneys. They each held out for $150,000. When Jerry heard the amount, he dug in his heels and said he'd quit the law if he couldn't break down two teenagers on the stand."

The trial dragged on for months. Flynn appeared more amused than annoyed by the lurid headlines and intimate details. Guess the swashbuckler was a better actor than anybody knew. Rose says, in private, Flynn was furious at being set up. And being branded a child molester made him sick. He was depressed about the shame he'd brought to his family. And he was scared—scared he'd lose, scared he'd have to do time, scared his career was ruined. "He needed a great deal of handholding during the torturous ordeal. He never fully recovered from the effects."

Flynn never had to sweat his career. His fan mail increased fivefold during the trial and for the first time in months, the war was pushed off the front pages. Within weeks, Warner's top publicist had the whole country wishing they were "in like Flynn." It became a national catch-phrase.

In the courtroom, Geisler lived up to his legend, cleverly discrediting the girls. Details

Errol toasts Nora, his bride-to-be. They met during his rape trial. She sold candy at the courthouse (January 1943).

of their seductions became unintentionally hilarious. They dressed in school clothes, pigtails, and bobby socks, but it didn't take a genius to see these girls had been around the block . . . a few times. No doubt they both slept with Flynn when they were underage, but no one seemed to care. C'mon, boys will be boys. After five long months, Flynn was acquitted of all charges in just under four hours. Terrified the verdict could go the other way, Flynn had a private plane waiting at the airport for a quick getaway. "Happily," says Rose, "it never came to that."

Flynn got off lucky. Nobody could be that lucky twice, and Geisler knew it. That's why when the second frame-up came months later, he told Warner to pay it. There were two more girls, one pregnant, the other a minor. And this time, they held Warner up for five times as much. Late one night, Rose delivered $50,000 in a suitcase to a woman in exchange for a deposition signed by both

A victory handshake with Geisler and Robert Ford (February 8, 1943).

girls that did not mention Flynn. The public would never know what it was really like to be "in like Flynn" . . . until now.

Flynn and drinking pals like John Barrymore, W. C. Fields, and Dave Chasen gathered at Don the Beachcomber's to celebrate life. Don himself is said to have created the drink to relieve a patron's hangover. The customer returned the next day and said the drink had made him feel like a zombie. Don managed to get six types of rum in his drink. We offer four.

The Zombie

1½	ounces dark rum (86 proof)
¾	ounce Jamaica rum (90 proof)
¾	ounce light rum (86 proof)
¾	ounce pineapple juice
¾	ounce papaya juice
1	ounce lime juice
	Pineapple wheel and cherry for garnish
	Demerara rum (151 proof)
1	teaspoon powdered sugar

In a glass with ice combine the dark rum, Jamaica rum, light rum, pineapple juice, papaya juice, and lime juice. Shake. Strain into a chilled pint or hurricane glass. Garnish with a pineapple wheel and a cherry. Float Demerara rum and sprinkle powdered sugar on top.

Dorothy Kilgallen

Some people think Dorothy Kilgallen was just a gossip columnist. They don't know anything. Dorothy was a newspaperwoman all the way, determined, courageous, and outspoken. It made her the best. It got her killed.

Dorothy came up the hard way, determined to make good in the man's world of newspaper reporting. She wasn't the type of woman you usually find in a newsroom—no smell of coffee and cigarettes about her, just perfume. But her soft, quiet ways hid a strong will, a sharp mind, and driving ambition. She was a born newspaperwoman. She loved the business, the action. She learned to flirt, lie, or plead her way into an interview, and when that failed she sometimes broke in, climbing through basement windows—white gloves, high heels, and all. She wrote the same way: exciting, imaginative, and distinctly feminine.

Dorothy started as a Hearst "sob sister" in 1931, but murder cases became her strong suit. Her most outstanding coverage was of the Sam Sheppard trial, the doctor accused of his wife's murder, later the basis for *The Fugitive*. But it was "The Voice of Broadway," her *New York Journal-American* column, that made Kilgallen the most powerful woman reporter in the country. She was a Broadway columnist who could make or break a reputation with a word, and a radio and television personality known to millions. In 1940, she married actor/producer Richard Kollmar, a handsome WASP with a pedigree. They produced three children and, for nearly two decades, they hosted WOR Radio's *Breakfast with Dorothy and Dick,* where they dished up last night's social scene with the morning coffee; pass the sugar, please. But most of Dick's solo projects failed. Dwarfed by Dorothy's success, he drank, took pills, and turned into a wholly pathetic figure.

Dorothy's fall from the heights started as a feud with Frank Sinatra. The two began as friends, but Dorothy turned on him, relentlessly sniping at him for years. Once, she published his address. When he moved, she published it again. She was asking for it, and Frank, pushed to the edge, decided to let her have it. During his acts in New York and Vegas, he got nasty, calling her an ugly broad, comparing her to a chipmunk. His nickname for her, "Chinless Wonder," stuck with Dorothy till the day she died. All the folks she'd been tough on laughed long and hard at Frank's jokes. Kilgallen was down for the count.

But this dame hated to

lose. Estranged from her husband, starved for affection, she drank, took pills, and surprised everyone—even herself—by jumping into the most passionate affair of her life. "Sob King" Johnnie Ray was fifteen years younger and a homosexual—except that he flipped over Dorothy. He was just what the doctor ordered. Dorothy came around. Secretly, she began to fight her addiction to booze and pills. The roller-coaster ride of passion, power, and pills was over. In Switzerland, she took "the cure" and came back sharp, clear, and ready for the biggest story of her life. She got it.

In 1964, Dorothy covered another murder trial—Jack Ruby, the Dallas club owner who plugged Lee Harvey Oswald while half the police force—and the whole country—watched. Hell, they held the poor bastard up as a target. JFK's alleged assassin was silenced before he could talk. Dorothy smelled a rat. She talked her way into a private interview with Ruby—the only reporter able to pull that off. They spoke for six minutes. Afterward, she flew to New Orleans. Later, that city figured big in the assassination conspiracy theory, but nobody knew it then. Ruby had let something slip, alright. Back in New York, she dug further and linked the recent death of Marilyn Monroe to Kennedy. Someone on or near the Warren Commission, investigating the assassination, leaked information to her. She wrote columns that enflamed the Commission, whose members argued Oswald was a lone gunman. Kilgallen was on to something big, and she knew it. She told friends she was going to bust the Kennedy assassination wide open. Three weeks later she was dead.

Dorothy was found about noon on Monday, November 8, 1965, sitting up in bed with a book. She couldn't read without glasses, but they weren't on, they weren't even near her. She'd already read the book propped open on her lap; she never read books twice. More than fifteen hours after her weekly television appearance on *What's My Line?*, she was still wearing heavy makeup from her chest up, including false eyelashes. No woman would go to bed like that. Death came from alcohol and barbiturate poisoning. Next to the bed was a water glass laced with barbiturates—fifteen to twenty pills according to the autopsy. That's too few for suicide and too many for an accidental overdose, just enough to kill her. A dozen people, including Joan Crawford, were all over that bedroom before the police were ever called. Any notes and papers she had on Ruby, Monroe, and Kennedy disappeared.

Dorothy loved a good vodka and tonic. After completing her final What's My Line? *broadcast, she and a friend went for drinks at P. J. Clark's. At 1:00 A.M., she walked into the cocktail lounge of the Regency Hotel to meet her latest lover. She passed a friend on the way to a corner table. He left at 1:30 and said Dorothy was still there. He's the last person to admit seeing her alive.*

Vodka Tonic à la the Regency Hotel

2	ounces vodka
4	ounces tonic water
	Lime wedge for garnish

Fill a highball glass with ice and pour in the vodka. Fill with tonic water. Stir, and garnish with a lime wedge.

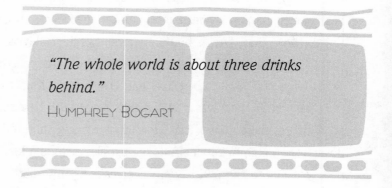

"The whole world is about three drinks behind."

HUMPHREY BOGART

Hors D'Oeuvres and Soup and Salad

Clara Bow 87

The Black Dahlia 95

Bing Crosby 101

Phil Spector 107

Clara Bow

Sincerely Clara Bow

It began as a feud between two girlfriends. When it was over, one was in jail and the other—one of the world's biggest stars—lay in a sanatorium, her career in ruins, her spirit broken. So what happened?

Clara Bow was just the snap in the garters the world needed after WWI. The bouncy redhead symbolized the ultimate jazz baby of the Roaring Twenties, the "IT" girl. Man, did she sizzle, but no femme fatale here. Clara was a fun-loving, generous, loyal pal who was more at home with working people than high-flung society types. She played poker with the boys on the crew and hired a studio hairdresser to be her live-in secretary. And the Brooklyn Bonfire was not afraid to pass around some success. She helped pal Gary Cooper get noticed, and Jean Harlow, too. Not many stars had that kind of security. But Clara, she was all about sharing the wealth.

Women loved her because she was so liberated, so modern. They bobbed their hair,

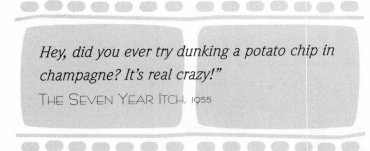

Hey, did you ever try dunking a potato chip in champagne? It's real crazy!"
THE SEVEN YEAR ITCH, 1955

went without underwear, and tried to give their lips Clara's bee-stung look. And if you gotta be told why men loved her, I feel sorry for ya. There were plenty of 'em, too: movie stars and movie extras, millionaires and college boys. One man said she kissed him so hard his lips bled and ached for days. When Clara kissed you, oh brother, you stayed kissed. Theater owners also loved Clara, voting her their Favorite Cinema Star. She worked hard for that title, cranking out the pictures and publicity. Her fan mail was voluminous: In 1927, she received more mail than the average town of five thousand people.

It looked like all fun and games, but it was a lot of pressure for a girl of twenty-two. There were little breakdowns along the way, followed by binge eating and binge sex. "I think wildly gay people are usually hiding from something in themselves," she told a reporter. "The best life has taught them is to snatch at every moment of fun and excitement, because they feel sure fate is going to hit them over the head with a club at the first opportunity." How could Clara know anything about that? That ain't the half of it.

Clara appeared to be a free spirit, but she wasn't free. She was a captive of a torturous childhood, of physical, emotional, and sexual abuse heaped on her by her disturbed parents. Her father raped her. Her deranged mother tried to kill her. These things happened on a regular basis. In between, she starved. A "new faces" contest in a movie magazine provided her escape. She turned the prize, a trip to Hollywood for a small film role, into super stardom in six years. The shop girls and secretaries she played in the movies were a big step up from the dire poverty of her youth in Brooklyn. The "wildly gay" pace was not about making new memories; it was about keeping the old ones at bay.

Daisy DeVoe, studio hairdresser at Paramount and Clara's devoted pal, came to live with her in '28 and for two years, the girls were like sisters. Daisy paid the bills, kept the house running, and rushed to Clara's side for parties or problems any time of day or night.

Believe it or not, this is just
a wardrobe test shot.
Some folks love their work.

Clara goes
Dutch.

She kept hush-hush about Clara's lifestyle and, likewise, Clara kept the lid on Daisy's affair with ace cameraman James Wong Howe, an Asian. America wasn't ready for that yet. Even in Hollywood, they had to keep their romance a secret.

Everything was great till Clara got herself a serious boyfriend. That's when cowboy actor Rex Bell noticed that Daisy had been helping herself to Clara's bank account. $35,000 was missing, along with clothing, furs, jewels, silver, love letters, and telegrams. Clara couldn't believe it. Why, she'd have given Daisy the stuff if she'd asked for it. Friendship meant much more to her than a fur coat. How could she pull a double cross like this? Before the girls could work things out, Rex fired Daisy. Daisy wanted to talk to Clara and threatened blackmail. That's when Clara told her to scram for good. Daisy didn't get sore; she got even, authoring a tell-all book available at every newsstand. *The Secret Love Life of Clara Bow* was secret no more. Turns out Clara was the sweetest little nymphomaniac you'd ever hope to know, devouring one, two, sometimes three men a night to satisfy her insatiable appetite. In the Roaring Twenties, Clara's behavior seemed like good, clean fun. Everybody was makin' whoopee. Then things changed. The stock market crashed. People were jumping out of windows. In 1931, Clara's fans lined up for bread instead of movies, and they had no sympathy for "two little Hollywood girls" who could misplace thousands of dollars without even noticing.

Clara tried to hold it together on the stand.

The press advance-billed Daisy's trial as "the most sensational since Fatty Arbuckle" and to make sure, they fanned the flames. In an actual media plot to get the "IT" girl, reporters were ordered to keep this story in the papers—at any cost. Even if public interest appeared to be wan-

The "IT" Café was more therapy than business venture for Clara.

ing, journalists were to harass conservative organizations to take a stand or bully small towns to ban Clara's films. "One of them would always chump for the publicity," one journalist said. "Then we could run with a headline: CLARA BOW'S FILMS BANNED IN TEXAS. The public didn't know it was some town of two hundred people." In this way, the media threw gasoline on a fading fire—and torched Clara Bow's career.

By the time court convened, thousands jammed the streets outside the courthouse, and thousands more bought daily extra editions. Daisy was ready for them. Nothing could ruffle her at the trial, not even when accused of "relieving" Clara of thousands of dollars. "If she had paid attention to business, I never would have taken a dime," Daisy reasoned. "She put me in a position to take anything I wanted . . . I was gonna tell her later. . . ." Gee, Daisy, that's tough.

Daisy wasn't goin' over for it alone. Clara was goin' with her. She spilled it all: the booz-

"And then I had a restful, nice luncheon . . . with four lawyers. On the eighty-eighth floor of the Watson's building. You know, the sky club. A cloud floated right into my soup plate."
DINNER AT EIGHT, 1933

After the breakdown, Clara packed on the pounds.

ing, the gambling, Clara's wild and wanton nights, and the squandering of huge sums of money. As Americans faced the dark depression, they considered this the worst sin of all.

Then it was Clara's turn, but instead of the spirited "IT" girl, a small, terrified woman, clinging to Rex Bell, slipped into the room. Trembling, uncertain, she looked guilty all over. On the stand, things got worse. Clara was a silent star. When the packed courtroom "gotta loada da" Brooklyn Bonfire's twang, they gave her the Bronx cheer, hooting and laughing until she slowly came apart at the seams. They fell silent when she completely broke down. Daisy was found guilty and got eighteen months in the slammer. Clara got life—and not the life she'd bargained for.

Paramount Studios, more than a little tired of bailing out their troublesome star and sensing the winds of change, left Clara to swing in the breeze. Abandoned by her studio, betrayed by her fans, a relic of the past, Clara suffered a nervous breakdown. She retired in 1933 at the ripe old age of twenty-six and spent her last thirty-four years in and out of sanatoriums, a complete recluse.

And what of the press, who had created a mountain out of this molehill of a story and brought the world down on Clara's head? They moved on to the next story and never looked back. And the public never got wise to the trick.

For a short time, Clara was the star of the "IT" Café, across from the Brown Derby, near Hollywood and Vine. In season, she offered oysters. Oysters have a reputation as an aphrodisiac, something Clara did not need . . . but some of her tired partners may have. She never learned to cook but credited her cook with this delicious recipe.

Deviled Oysters on the Half Shell

1	pint oysters
1	tablespoon butter
3	spring onions
2	tablespoons flour
½	cup milk
¼	cup cream
½	teaspoon salt
⅛	teaspoon nutmeg
½	teaspoon prepared mustard
½	tablespoon Worcestershire sauce
2	mushroom caps, chopped
¼	teaspoon chopped parsley
1	egg yolk
	Buttered cracker crumbs

Wash and chop the oysters. In a saucepan heat the butter and cook the onions for three minutes, then add the flour and stir well until blended. Add the milk and cream. Bring to the boiling point and add the salt, nutmeg, prepared mustard, Worcestershire sauce, mushroom caps, and parsley. Let simmer for 12 minutes, then mix in the egg yolk and the oysters. Spoon the mixture into the deep halves of the oyster shells, cover with buttered cracker crumbs, and bake for 15 minutes. (Clara neglected to provide the oven temperature, but we suggest 400°.)

"I'll admit I may have seen better days . . . but I'm still not to be had for the price of a cocktail, like a salted peanut."
ALL ABOUT EVE, 1950

The Black Dahlia

The legend of Hollywood's Black Dahlia began in an open field one chilly January morning in 1947. A passerby discovered the dismembered body of a young woman. Elizabeth Short was just twenty-two, from a small town outside Boston. Her flair for the dramatic—dyed jet-black hair and black clothing—earned her the nickname Black Dahlia among her pals. She came to L.A. with hopes for an acting career and instead became the victim of one of the city's most gruesome unsolved murders. Betty Short became a symbol for all the pretty girls from all the small towns who come to Hollywood with big dreams. Almost as soon as her body was found, reporters began to spin the tale of the mysterious starlet with the raven-black hair. How did a good girl get mixed up with the cookie who did this? Did the East Coast beauty go on a date with the wrong guy? She seemed mysterious, a bit of a tease. Some say she wasn't able to have sex and maybe led on the wrong

Above: This never-before-published portrait of Elizabeth Short was sent to Janice Knowlton by the late Detective Thad Stephan, who took it from her file.

George Knowlton, 1946, six months before he killed Elizabeth Short.

guy. Her mother said she never was in any trouble; habitués of the If Club, a lesbian bar near Seventh and Vermont, said different. All that sells papers, but that ain't the way it went down—not according to an eyewitness.

Elizabeth Short was one twisted sister. In her behalf, I will say that she must have suffered through a lot of abuse in her short life because you don't just put on a dog collar, get down on all fours, and bark like a dog for men outta nowhere. Maybe she tried to get into the movies for five minutes because she did meet Norma Jean Dougherty in a bar, another desperate, hungry, young wanna-be actress who'd been sexually abused, and they turned a couple of tricks together. Marilyn just wanted to pay the rent between gigs. She quickly saw that Betty was into much darker stuff. Marilyn hightailed it outta there and never looked back.

No, Betty Short was plain evil. A lot had to do with the monster she had an affair with for years, one George Knowlton, thirteen years her senior. What a piece of work he was. He met a teenage Betty on the East Coast, and when he moved across the country with his family, Betty traveled across country, too. And another interesting thing. Whatever city George and his family stayed in, a woman matching his mother's fair skin and dark hair died a horrible death. See, George was psycho, a vicious serial killer who hated his mother but couldn't do the deed to her, so he killed women who looked like her . . . lots of women. His daughter, Janice, remembers her father driving her around until he found a woman alone. He looked safe—a man and his little girl. So the woman walked off with George and a half-hour later, only George returned, lotta times, lotta towns.

In L.A., George worked for the mob in a low-level position, running numbers and money for the gambling boats off Long Beach. The cops knew George and his tan LaSalle—a poor man's Caddy, they called it. A lot of cops knew Betty, too, knew her real well. Most of them also knew that George and Betty had a little business together—a child prostitution ring out of an apartment at the Hawthorne Hotel near Hollywood Boulevard. George sold his own daughter, Janice, to pedophiles. "Aunt Betty" would slip her a glass of watered-down wine or a pill so she'd struggle less. Once, a cop came to the apartment and Janice thought, "I'm saved! Help is here!" until Betty unzipped the flatfoot's pants. Janice remembers the names of some of these johns . . . famous citizens of Los Angeles, a few names that would bring the Social Register to its knees; it appears some of them were there already. That is why Betty Short's murder was never solved. No one—not the cops, not the *L.A. Times,* not the studios—no one wanted anybody digging into that girl's life. There's a reason Hollywood's most famous or infamous murders don't get solved: big money.

So here's what happened. Betty got knocked up. She accused George and a bunch of her johns of being the heel. She made a lot of people mad . . . and nervous. She got scared and hid out for a while in Pacific Beach, south of La Jolla. Around that time, she got picked up for prostitution, and her blood test showed she was taking quinine sulfate, a remedy for her little "problem." When her welcome wore out in

George in 1956.

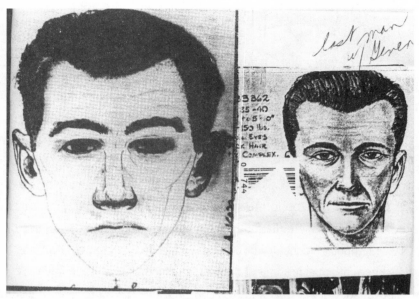

Two sketches of the man last seen with author James Elroy's mother in 1958.

San Diego, she bummed a ride back to L.A. Weak and sick, she got hold of George. He put her up in a small room at the rear of his garage. She miscarried the baby in a chamber pot.

Betty turned manic, loud, and out of control. She went into the house and took a bath. George's wife hit the roof and demanded he get rid of her. George was understandably ticked off. Back in the garage, he grabbed Betty by the throat and lifted her off the floor. He threw her down on a metal cot and tied her up at the wrists, the ankles, and put a noose around her neck. He left her there Friday night and all day Saturday till well past sunset. Finally, his rage was spent. That's when he reached for his hunting knife, the one he used to butcher deer. It was time for this bitch to shove off. He reached over her head to cut the rope at her wrists, but when Betty saw the knife, she gasped and jerked away. George gashed the right side of her face, severing the muscles in her cheek. The blade continued through her open mouth, slicing her left cheek as well. Janice went into shock. Betty looked bad, real bad. She began to choke on the blood. He cut the ropes, lifted her to a sitting position, and shoved a towel at her. He said it was an accident.

"It's nothin'," he told her. "I'll drive you to the hospital and they'll sew you up." But

George wasn't going to a hospital. Too many questions. He turned on the radio. *The Lone Ranger* was just starting, and the "William Tell Overture" filled the room. Betty was rocking back and forth, looking at the bloody towel. She didn't have the strength to run away or resist when George came toward her with another rope. He tied her hands behind her back. A bare light bulb lit the ghoulish, sagging flesh of her once-pretty face. She watched George take a hammer from his workbench, raise it above his head, and bring it down hard on her forehead. Betty slumped forward, motionless. Janice, in a trance, crumpled to the floor, pushing back from the horrible scene. Unbelievably, Betty lifted her face, forehead bloody, eyes swimming in her head. As the "Overture" reached its final crescendo, George brought the hammer down again, killing her. Then he used his Skil saw to cut her in half. He mutilated her corpse while telling Janice that if she ever told, she'd get the same treatment. Later, he made her fix Betty's hair for "her funeral."

Short told the last people she saw she was seeing George, who lived in Texas. She couldn't tell them George was married with six kids and lived on Texas Street, could she? But that shouldn't have stumped the authorities. Besides, George and Betty had been seen together—with Janice—all over, from San Pedro to Long Beach to the Hawthorne. But the cops never pulled George in. Matter of fact, every time a detective started to get somewhere with the case, he got pulled off, even under protest.

Former L.A. Sheriff's Deputy Donald Gibson was handed the Black Dahlia file by his superior in '49 when he joined the department. There were instructions: Don't delve into it, and "don't let anything concrete surface." Gibson told Janice he saw her father's name in the file along with names of powerful people in industry and show business. Now Janice believes her father meant to kill Betty—on orders from some of those powerful people . . . shades of her old acquaintance, Marilyn Monroe.

Author James Elroy's mother was murdered in 1958; he was ten. He

> *"FBI, CIA, ONI . . . we're all in the same alphabet soup."*
> NORTH BY NORTHWEST, 1959

believes it was the same man who murdered the Black Dahlia. He's right. Look at the sketches of the man his mother, Geneva, was last seen with (page 98), and look at George Knowlton (page 96). You gonna tell me cops who knew George Knowlton didn't recognize him? Yeah, and I got some oil wells on La Cienega to sell you. . . .

Janice remembers two recipes from her torturous days with the Black Dahlia. "I had a flashback of 'Aunt Betty,' in the one-bedroom Hawthorne apartment preparing this version of hurried corn chowder and feeding it to her hungry captive—me at age nine.

"The second recipe was from a john, a man who arrived at the Hawthorne with a bag of groceries and red wine. He ran his hands over his dark, slicked-back hair, put on one of those big white chef's aprons up to his armpits, and proceeded to show me how to make marinara sauce. As he tasted it, he told me, 'You don't have to add sugar if the tomatoes are ripe and sweet enough.' Then he went into the bedroom where 'Aunt Betty' was sleeping off her drugs, had sex with her in my presence, and molested me as well."

Janice adds, "I described this memory to Deputy Gibson. He told me my description fit 'to a T' the owner of an Italian restaurant on Hollywood Boulevard, a man known for dropping in places and cooking a meal."

Aunt Betty's Corn Chowder

| 1 | can creamed or kernel corn |
| 1 | glass milk |

Heat and serve.

A "John's" Marinara Sauce

Olive oil
Ripe tomatoes, peeled and cut up
Fresh chopped basil
Garlic

In a saucepan heat the olive oil and sauté the ingredients. You don't have to add sugar if the tomatoes are ripe and sweet enough. Serve over pasta.

Bing Crosby

Bing Crosby did it all . . . a world-class crooner whose baby blues and buh-buh-buh-boos made women weak in the knees. He was an award-winning dramatic actor, comedian, and beloved member of the Hollywood community.

Singer and *White Christmas* costar Rosemary Clooney: "Bing had great personal dignity and reserve, which was often hard to penetrate."

This pipe-smoking, golfing, horseracing, king of the *Road* pictures with best pal Bob Hope appeared humble, charming, and easygoing. His success seemed effortless.

Road pictures costar Dorothy Lamour: "There were times when, for short intervals, I would feel very close to Bing. Then there were other times when I felt that he looked upon me as a complete stranger. . . . As I look back, I think he was a very shy, insecure man. The world looked upon him as one of the great talents. He just never saw himself in that light."

Above: Bing and the boys, May '54:
Gary and Phillip, up top, survived. Dennis
and Lindsay would kill themselves.

Bing: the King of Sing.

Everything Crosby touched turned to gold. He starred in fifty-seven films, sold more than 300 million records, and earned top-dollar for years as a radio, television, and nightclub performer.

"He was a tough guy," said bandleader Phil Harris. "Make one wrong move, and he'd never speak to you again."

And oh yeah, he was a family man. Everybody knew Bing's four boys.

"My situation as a father is maybe a bit more complicated than . . . most dads'," Crosby explained in his autobiography, *Call Me Lucky.* "Raising the sons of a movie star presents special problems. When the children of people prominent in show business go to school or to entertainments or to parties, the solid, well-grounded kids they meet at those places pay them no special attention, but there's always a bunch of bubbleheads who make a fuss over a boy whose father or mother's name is known in the entertainment world. 'With all the money your old man's got, you'll never have to work,' they tell him. Or, 'You mean you've got only one car?' and they ladle out the old goo. If the kid who gets this treatment is a little susceptible—as some of mine are—such guff can spoil them. My slant on such buttering up is this: There's an old Italian proverb that says, 'Never kiss a baby unless he's asleep.' When I want to be especially flattering to one of my offspring, I say, 'Nice going,' and let it go at that."

"He cared deeply. He just had a rough time showing it," said his oldest son, Gary. What an understatement.

"There have been times when I couldn't tell whether I was Captain Bligh in a Hawaiian sport shirt or the cream puff of the world," Bing continued, "for Dixie used to tell me that I was too lax. . . . Lax or not, I'll bet they remember the spankings they got when they were younger. I laid in a big leather belt. . . . They remember that alright."

"The old man believed what he believed, and he thought he was doing right," Gary wrote in his own autobiography, *Going My Own Way.* "He wasn't any tougher than a lot of fathers of his generation. And a lot of kids can handle that kind of upbringing without any difficulty. It was too bad that my brothers and I didn't buy it and turn out the way he wanted. That would have made it very comfortable for everyone. But whatever the reasons, we didn't. Lindsay and the twins clammed up like a shell. I bulled my neck and fought him tooth and nail all the way down the line. To my own destruction. The discipline just didn't work with us."

Seems der Bingle was der Bungler as a dad. His strict regimen of humiliation and brutality left all the boys damaged. Gary was the only one who spoke publicly of the abuse—and the only one who managed to get sober. "If we left anything in our room—a pair of socks, underwear—he made us wear it to school on a string around our necks. And he'd call the teacher to make sure we didn't take it off." Bing didn't want any spoiled brats in his family, so he bent over backward to prevent it. Wait, that's wrong; he bent them over two or three times a week to make sure that didn't happen. "Our housekeeper was allowed to whip us . . . Mom whipped us . . . Dad used to give it to us with a Western leather belt that had little silver points sticking out. He'd take our pants down and calmly whip us till we bled . . . when we got older, he used a chain or a big cane."

What a guy. He's crooning away, trotting these kids out for Christmas television specials, then he lines them up at home and uses that famous golf swing of his on their backsides. Ba-ba-ba-BOOM, der Bingle. The kids never got an apology or a penny of his $80 million fortune. Once, after Bing had remarried and started a new family, he told a reporter that he was leaving the discipline to his wife. He thought he might have been too strict with the boys. Gee, ya think? All four were plagued by drug and alcohol problems and manic depression, and two committed suicide. That's quite an inheritance.

Bing picked up this recipe for seafood cocktail in Baja California. He had a hacienda at Las Cruces where he often went deep-sea fishing during the "Golden Age" of Baja's fishing resorts, between 1952 and 1970. Many claimed it was the best bill fishing in the entire world. Hemingway went there; so did John Wayne, Desi Arnaz, Clark Gable, and a small gang of other celebrity sportsmen who called it "fishing with a vengeance."

Ceviche

seafood cocktail

1½	pounds white fillets of fish
	Juice of 9 limes
1	large onion, minced fine
16	large green olives, cut up
2	tablespoons juice from olive jar
3	medium tomatoes, peeled and minced fine with juice

¾	cup ketchup or Mexican red sauce
½	cup olive oil
1	teaspoon oregano
2	teaspoons salt
5	dashes Salsa picante (hot sauce)

Cut the fish into cubes or squares. Soak in lime juice for 90 minutes. Put in a sieve and rinse well. Mix with the other ingredients and chill. The lime juice does the cooking.

"My simple child reaction of what you did is that you are not funny. Funnier than you is even Stuart Schlossmen, who is my friend, and is eleven, and puts walnuts in his mouth and makes noises. What is not funny is to call us names, and what is mostly not funny is how sad you are, and I'd feel sorry for you if it wasn't for how dull you are. And those are the worst-tasting potato chips that I've ever tasted. And that's my opinion from the blue, blue sky."

A THOUSAND CLOWNS, 1965

Phil Spector

Early on a February morning, 2003, a black Mercedes made its way to the outskirts of L.A., a town called Alhambra. The streets were empty at that hour, the working-class townfolk tucked into their beds. The car slowly climbed the long driveway toward a mansion named Pyrenees Castle, a little much for the neighborhood, but cheaper than buying in the city. The owner of both the house and the car was in the back seat, accompanied by a woman he'd met earlier that evening. The man told the driver to wait with the car to take the woman home. The couple entered the foyer of the thirty-three-room home. Some time later, neighbors and the driver heard gunshots. The driver leaped from the car and bolted for the house. In the entryway, he saw the woman sprawled in a pool of blood. She'd been shot in the face. The man and a gun were nearby. No one else was in the house. The driver called 911.

The man was rich, eccentric, and yesterday's news—record producer Phil Spector,

Above: Spector played a coke dealer in
Easy Rider (1969).

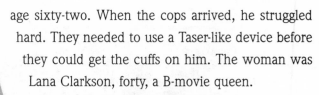

age sixty-two. When the cops arrived, he struggled hard. They needed to use a Taser-like device before they could get the cuffs on him. The woman was Lana Clarkson, forty, a B-movie queen.

"Lana was a beautiful woman, a wonderful actress and an adventurous spirit," said cult director Roger Corman. A knockout at six feet tall and built, she starred as Corman's *Barbarian Queen.* Ms. Clarkson had many qualities, among them bravery. Corman told the press, "[S]he performed all of her own stunts and showed unusual fortitude and athleticism in her horseback-riding and fight sequences." The girl could take care of herself.

Lana's friends said she was beautiful inside, too: kind, spiritual, with a positive outlook—even after an accident the year before that had left her unable to work. Lana fell while dancing with children at a Christmas party and broke both her wrists. Most of 2002 was spent in recovery and rehabilitation. Though some called them "hard times," Lana was characteristically optimistic. She took classes and worked comic book and film conventions, making quick cash signing autographs and posing with her fans. Still, she couldn't make ends meet. For the first time in twenty years, she needed "civilian" work. A hostess gig at the House of Blues would keep her days free. She told friends maybe she'd make some new connections. She connected, alright.

Phil Spector was nine when his father committed suicide. The inscription on his tombstone was "To know him is to love him." Spector used it as the title for his first hit record. *Rolling Stone* magazine called what came after "songs that last three minutes and forever": the Ronettes' "Be My Baby," the Crystals' "Da Doo Ron Ron," the Righteous Brothers' "You've Lost That Lovin' Feeling." Spector and his fabled Wrecking Crew—a group of session musicians featuring Glen Campbell, Leon Russell, and assistant producer and backup singer Sonny Bono—created the vast and mighty "Wall of Sound," distinguished by lofty orchestration and multilayered vocals. Baby, it was something else.

In the 1970s, Spector produced the Beatles' *Let It Be* album, George Harrison's *All Things Must Pass* album, and John Lennon's *Imagine* album. He won two Grammys and a place among pop music legends. But to know Phil Spector was not to love him. What a screwball.

Ronnie Spector, lead singer of the Ronettes and Phil's second wife, lived in constant terror during their four-year marriage. His sons tell of being locked in their rooms, of forced sexual activity with women, of verbal and mental cruelty. "If you looked up 'controlling' in the dictionary, his picture would probably be there," said son Donte in an exclusive interview for *Extra*. And then there were the guns. Everybody knew he loved guns. There were plenty of stories about him pulling a piece on Ronnie, the Ramones, John Lennon, and more. When he drank, things got really scary.

"I would say I'm probably relatively insane, to an extent," Spector told Mick Brown of the *London Telegraph* just a month after Clarkson's death. "I take medication for schizophrenia. . . . I have a bipolar personality,

> *"Cockeye cook did it, him and two of his meatballs."*
> SLAUGHTER ON TENTH AVENUE, 1957

which is strange. I'm my own worst enemy. I have devils inside that fight me. . . . I wasn't well enough to function as a regular part of society, so I chose not to." Spector retreated to the safety of his castle and gave up the booze. But lately, he had started drinking again. He was feeling better, trying to get out more. Hindsight's 20/20. He should've stayed home.

After midnight on Sunday, February 2, 2003, Spector and a woman friend arrived at Dan Tana's restaurant for dinner. He was a regular, and they sat at his usual table away from the door. A customer recognized him, said he was rumpled and sweaty and kept going to the bathroom. He ordered a drink. Then another. Spector hadn't ordered a drink for years, so the bartender delivered the second one himself. He asked if everything was OK, and Spector told him he was fine. The bill came to $55, $33 of it for liquor. He left a $500 tip and split around 1:30. Spector arrived at the House of Blues alone. He went upstairs to their members-only club-within-the-club, the Foundation Room. Phil downed a daiquiri, ordered a $250 bottle of champagne, and chased the bubbly with whiskey. Before 2:00 A.M. Lana joined his group.

Spector and Clarkson left the Foundation Room at 2:00 A.M. and were seen talking in the parking lot. At 3:00, they both got into his Mercedes. The chauffeur isn't saying much, only that they drove around, then headed for Alhambra. At 5:00 A.M., he heard the shots.

They booked Spector on suspicion of first-degree murder, but months passed with no charges filed. He was out on a million dollars bail, saying Lana's death was accidental suicide and he'd soon be cleared. "If we had come to a conclusion as monumental as suicide, we would have a duty to say so publicly," Sheriff's Capt. Frank Merriman told the Associated Press. "We believe a crime occurred." He denied reports Spector's name would soon be cleared. "No one involved in this investigation said that. My opinion is that somebody is orchestrating this to plant seeds of doubt with potential jurors."

Spector hired O. J. Simpson "Dream Team" attorney Robert Shapiro, who responded, "I am convinced that the thorough and accurate investigation of the evidence by the Los Angeles Sheriff's Department, its criminalists, and the County Coroner will prove that Phil Spector is innocent of any crime." Cops weren't looking at anybody else.

How did Spector walk away? How was everything kept so quiet? What were the police waiting for? This was a case for the books, a Hollywood murder with no leaks.

Weeks later, Spector was back at Dan Tana's, this time with four young dolls. Each one used her cell phone to call the tabloids. Seems they wanted to make the morning papers. There was such a mob scene out front, Phil sneaked out through the kitchen. He left a $500 tip. Life as usual for the producer. Family and friends of Lana Clarkson wait. And hope for justice.

Dan Tana's Italian restaurant in West Hollywood has been open for business for thirty-eight years. A favorite hangout for show-biz types, it's old-fashioned—dark, checked tablecloths, wine bottles hanging from the ceiling. On the night of the crime, Spector requested his usual spot, table number four, farthest from the entrance. He ordered the Tana salad.

Tana Salad

Bite-size pieces of:
Mozzarella cheese
Bell peppers
Garbanzos
Tomatoes
Cucumbers
Lettuce

Toss all ingredients with your favorite Italian dressing.

Main Dishes

Cheiro 115

Rudolph Valentino 121

Mary Astor 129

Clara Blandick 133

Benjamin "Bugsy" Siegel 137

Joan Crawford...141

Robert Mitchum 145

Lana Turner 149

John Wayne...155

Marilyn Monroe 159

Frank Sinatra 165

Sal Mineo 169

Sharon Tate 173

Liberace 179

Natalie Wood 183

Nicole Brown Simpson 189

Robert Blake 193

Cheiro

Who's *Who* listed him as Count Louis Hamon, a relative of the first Duke of Normandy, no less. Back in Ireland where he was born in 1866, they called him William John Warner; that's probably more like it. But to the world, he was Cheiro—hands down the world's greatest palmist.

Bill was a good-looker, full of adventure. His mother, a French dish, had the gift of a sixth sense. Bill had it too. Around fourteen, he left home to work in England, but felt the call of the Far East. In Bombay, he studied with masters of the occult and palmistry. That's when he changed his name to Cheiro—Greek for "hand." Back in London, he opened a Turkish consulting room on Bond Street in 1890. Word spread fast. Within weeks, he was holding hands with Europe's most celebrated citizens.

Not everyone was a believer. During that first year, some of Cheiro's clients put him to the test to see if he was on the level. One of these clients held out a pair of flabby hands from behind a curtain. "You're a famous man at the very height of your success," Cheiro told him. "However, your lines of fate and success are broken just seven years farther on. You must beware of taking any precipitate action then. If you do, it will be the ruin of you."

The man stood up and threw back the curtain. "My dear Cheiro, the mystery of the world is the visible, not the invisible." Playwright Oscar Wilde announced to his friends, "Cheiro may be right; but, as fate keeps no road-menders on her highways—Que sera sera!—What will be will be."

Seven years and two ugly trials later, Wilde went to prison for homosexual practices. Released in 1897, sick, broke, despised, Wilde lived under an assumed name in bitterness and despair until his death three years later. Cheiro said it didn't have to go down that way. He never claimed his predictions were written in stone. Sometimes they're a warning, but Wilde gave them the air. "This otherwise clever man could not realize the road-menders were present within himself," Cheiro later wrote about Wilde. "He made no change in his habits and so went headlong to his doom."

A traveling man, in 1893 Cheiro felt ready to take on the States; that meant New York. New Yorkers are a tough crowd. The press came up with a test: thirteen palm prints from prominent New Yorkers. They defied him to identify the owners. Cheiro was damned either way—a mistake would finish him in the United States, but he had to agree to it. He labored half the night and hell if he didn't hit the jackpot: thirteen out of thirteen, including the mayor, the district attorney, soprano Lillian Russell, and poetess Ella Wheeler Wilcox.

The print that gave Cheiro the most trouble belonged to Dr. Henry Meyer, a murderer in Sing Sing. He was supposed to be executed in the electric chair in a week. Cheiro said the guy wouldn't burn. "He will live for years, but in prison." The day got closer and all of New York waited to see if the great Cheiro would finally fall on his face. "Day after day went past with no news to relieve the tension," he wrote in his memoirs. "The evening papers, full of details of the preparations for the execution fixed for the next morning, were eagerly brought up. I bought one and read every line. Midnight came. Suddenly boys rushed through the streets screaming 'Special edition!' I read across the front page 'Meyer Escapes the Chair. Supreme Court Finds Flaw in Indictment.' The miracle had happened; the sentence was altered to imprisonment for life."

The Big Apple declared Cheiro "the eighth wonder of the world," and his business boomed. Everybody who was anybody consulted him, including President Grover Cleveland and writer Mark Twain, who signed the visitor's book this way: "Cheiro exposed my character with humiliating accuracy. I ought not to confess this accuracy, still I am moved to do so."

Cheiro made his reputation and big dough in the states, but he missed Europe. Back there, he saw lords and ladies; kings and queens like Leopold II of Belgium and Edward VII of England; and celebrated actresses Lily Langtree (Edward's mistress), Sarah Bernhardt, and Eleanora Duse. Cheiro had a way with dames; he must have to score with femme-fatale spy Mata Hari after he told her she'd meet a violent end. Now that's smooth.

In 1905, Cheiro sailed to St. Petersburg, Russia. The first guy through the door was a "strange, shabbily dressed man with a long dirty beard and piercing eyes." Rasputin, the "mad monk," was mean, too. His hold over the Czarina Alexandra would help destroy the monarchy. "Absolute evil filled the room when he entered," Cheiro wrote. "I told him he would rise to power and have great influence over the czar and his family."

"I know that," Rasputin snapped. "I want to know beyond that. Who will ultimately rule Russia? Czar Nicholas or myself?"

"Neither," Cheiro told him. "The czar will be shot by his own people in a great revolution. But you will already be dead by then." Rasputin was hopping mad, but Cheiro let him have it. "I see a vio-

"The murderer is right here in this room, sitting at this table. You may serve the fish."
THE THIN MAN, 1934

lent end for you in your own home. You will be stricken by poison, knife, and shot at. But even that will not be the end of you. While still alive, you will be taken in a sack and thrown into a frozen river. It is there that you will die, as the icy waters of the Neva close above your head."

Rasputin didn't take the news well. He went off like a Roman candle, cussing and yelling. He stared hard at him, trying to put the double whammy on Cheiro, who avoided the wild man's hypnotic glare. Finally, he stormed out. "It was my closest brush with death and the most weird and frightening interview I ever conducted." And get a load of this, the monk bought the farm in 1916 pretty much the way Cheiro said.

Cheiro traveled the world while writing books on palmistry, numerology, ghosts, fate, and marriage. (His books on palmistry are still the best out there, and Elvis lived by *Cheiro's Book of Numbers*.) In *Cheiro's World Predictions*, he figured the future like this:

"Some astounding inventions in relation to aerial navigation will be made in the United States. . . . The U.S. will grasp this opportunity to bring about the complete conquest of the air, which is foreshadowed by the eagle being the national emblem.

"Christianity will continue to decline and by 2150 will be only a minor sect without much influence.

"Armageddon will be fought on the plains of Palestine. . . . The pretext for the start of the War of Wars will be when the Israelites and their coworkers in Palestine open up Egypt with its vast resources. This will arouse antagonism from the followers of Islam, and Turkey, backed by Russia, will endeavor to recapture Palestine . . . Germany and England will ally and pour immense numbers of troops into Palestine and Egypt, against Russia and Turkey. In the end, when the smoke has cleared away, there will be a new and powerful nation of the Jews . . . the reunion of the twelve tribes . . . a wonderfully organized central government in Palestine will radiate laws of life and humanity to the entire world.

"The next age will be the Aquarian, in which women will emerge in new and undreamed-of greatness. 'The New Age' we are now commencing is a predestined period of time in which women have to come to the front in all matters of public life. There is no body of men who will be able for long to resist the tide of thought that for either good or evil is bringing women into power." A little ahead of his time, he predicted a woman president of the United States by 1980.

At fifty-four, the old bird was strong, still handsome, and "as wide as a grand piano" when he finally tied the knot. Six years later, he and his wife, Mena, moved into a large home on Hollywood Boulevard. The *L.A. Times* gave him the full treatment, calling him the "confidant and advisor of people whose names head the social, political, and financial registers of the world."

Celebrities fell all over themselves to get to him. A short interview was $100 and at times, he was so hot, appointments were auctioned for as much as $1,000. Douglas Fairbanks, Lillian Gish, Norma Talmadge, Ramon Novarro, Serge Eisenstein, Erich von Stroheim—only Charlie Chaplin refused to allow Cheiro a look at his hands. The rest of Hollywood sat at his feet.

"I waited long to meet the great Cheiro, and I can't tell you how wonderful this meeting has been for me," said America's Sweetheart, Mary Pickford, shortly after his arrival. "All through my early years, when going through those darkest moments, my courage was kept up by looking at the Line of Sun in his book *Cheiro's Language of the Hand*. From it, I knew that success would come and it did come—at exactly the date shown in the book."

With all that foresight, you can guess Cheiro saw his own end coming. He had a severe heart attack in June of '36 and lapsed in and out of a coma for months. During a conscious moment on Tuesday, October 6, he told Mena he would die at midnight on Thursday.

Mena, close to midnight, sat at her husband's bedside. Suddenly, their dog began howling. She couldn't quiet him. Then she heard the front door open and close. Footsteps came upstairs toward the bedroom. She wasn't afraid, not even when the door opened. She saw no one, but the room instantly filled with gusts of wind and a strong scent of roses. The clock struck the hour, not twelve strikes, but thirteen. With that, Cheiro breathed his last, and Mena heard a host of footsteps descend the stairs.

The story made page one of the *Times* the next day and was the subject of speculation in a large article in the *Sunday Times Magazine.* The footsteps, the wind, the roses—Cheiro's friends figured it this way: It was the mystic's welcome into the Great Beyond. The great traveler had left for his final journey. Pretty slick.

Cheiro picked up this recipe on his travels in Paris.

Fricassee of Chicken

First, to make the chicken tender, Cheiro recommends that you take it out of the hen-run, pursue it into the open country and, when you have made it run, kill it with a gun loaded with very small shot. The meat of the chicken, gripped with fright, will become tender. This method seems infallible even for the oldest and toughest hens.

Next, joint the chicken.

In a cast-iron cooking pot, before a good wood fire, cook lightly some pieces of bacon (¼ pound). When they are nicely golden, take them out and lightly cook the pieces of chicken. Mix them all up and sprinkle with flour (1 tablespoon) and generously with shallots (5) finely chopped with parsley. Salt, pepper, and cover. Let it simmer slowly and for a long time on a gentle heat (2 hours). Add a good glass of cognac (⅓ cup) half an hour before serving.

"Hey waitress, this steak's tough."

"Well, you can't send it back; you bit it."

THEY DRIVE BY NIGHT, 1940

Rudolph Valentino

On August 23, 1926, Rudolph Valentino suddenly died and the world went crazy. Hundreds of thousands of men and women caused a riot in the streets of New York City the day of his funeral. Same thing happened a week later in Los Angeles. Not just dames, but guys reportedly committed suicide, and rumors sprang up of a cult of the bizarre with strong necrophilic overtones, if you get my drift. This guy, Rudy, that's what his pals and his fans called him, was a phenomenon. I mean, you just looked at him and saw sex—hot and taboo, sister. They even named a condom after this guy. Fan magazines said he "drove men and women to despair," but it was for entirely different reasons. One thing's for certain, he changed sex in America forever.

The Valentino legend began in Castellaneta, Italy, with Rodolpho Alfonzo Rafaelo Pierre Filibert Guglielmi di Valentina d'Antonguolla, the middle child of an Italian army veterinarian and a French schoolteacher. Rodolpho's mama spoiled him rotten and he grew into the neighborhood bully. At twelve, when his father died, Rudy was shipped off to military school. He bounced to medical school, applied to the Royal Naval Academy (where he was refused admittance), and finally completed studies in agriculture and farming. Afterward, in 1912, he traveled to Paris, where he furthered his unofficial education in "social" studies.

At seventeen, Rudy embraced the excitement of the nightclubs and bars in the "City of Light" full-throttle. And he learned he could dance. Solid but graceful, he quickly mastered Apache dancing, a macho routine spiced up with smoldering looks and rough, menacing treatment of women. You'll take it and you'll like it, baby. He was born to it, and the style became the foundation for his on-screen love image. Already something of a "mama's boy," Rudy was also drawn to the gay underworld of pre-WWI Paris. He loved the dancing, the wild nightlife, and its uninhibited inhabitants. These distinctly different sides of his personality formed a cloud of sexual mystery that existed for the rest of his brief life.

Rudy and Natacha, 1925.

Late in 1913, Rodolpho Guglielmi arrived in New York, the land of opportunity. He worked as a gardener, dishwasher, busboy—and, on several occasions, was booked on suspicion of petty theft and blackmail. By night, the darkly handsome Rodolpho sought the comfort of the Broadway district and its dance halls. He learned the steamy tango and, as his dancing improved, he moved from busboy to taxi dancer, entertaining wealthy, unescorted women who tipped him generously hoping for more.

Rudy got a break when he replaced Clifton Webb (who also started as a dancer) as

His passionate performance in *Four Horsemen of the Apocalypse* made women faint.

the partner of pretty Bonnie Glass, a popular dancer. As a team, they could demand as much as $50 a week. But old habits die hard. It wasn't long before Rudy got himself arrested, and this time he spent a few days in one of New York's toughest detention centers, the Tombs. It was pretty rough, and when he was released, he left town right away with the cast of a musical. It folded in Utah. It took some time, but Rudy made his way to San Francisco, where he supported himself dancing—and whatever. In 1917, he arrived in Hollywood.

The movies did not sit up and take notice of Rudy. All he could get were extra and bit parts as exotic dancers or sneering villains. After three years, he was still only a minor player. He was typecast. Dark Latins made great villains. Heroes were all-American chest-thumpers like Douglas Fairbanks and Wally Reid. But the end of WWI brought big changes. Folks craved ragtime and romance. Valentino chased a little romance, too. In November of '19, he married an actress, Jean Acker, but she locked him out on their wedding night and the union was never consummated. Acker was rumored to be part of the "Sewing Circle," a lesbian group led by Nazimova, a dark and mysterious Russian who was big stuff at Metro. Nazimova held great influence over Rudy and arranged this marriage, although whom it helped is a mystery. Acker's career was further along than Rudy's, and her rejection crushed the poor guy. Never fear: Within a year, women everywhere would be at his feet. Valentino would be known as the "King of Romance."

Another of Rudy's mother images—the most important—was June Mathis, chief of Metro's (not yet MGM) script department. She was smart and powerful. Her opinion carried a lot of weight with the big guys. She convinced them to produce an antiwar epic, *The Four Horsemen of the Apocalypse.* It was Metro's first million-dollar production, and she convinced them to put the unknown Rudy in the lead. Mathis was a smart cookie. The movie was a huge hit, and, from his first moment on the screen, Valentino signaled the start of a whole new way to make love.

The awkward advances of the the shy boy-next-door types couldn't hold a candle to Rudy. He didn't just enter a room—he took it, striding masterfully across the floor with ease and grace. His brooding eyes and sensual mouth promised experience and skill. To tango or to kiss, when he bent his leading ladies back from the waist like lilies, dames everywhere gasped and surrendered. Valentino gave permission to fantasize about hot, forbidden sex, and American women especially were loud and clear in their response to him. They went ga-ga!

American men felt different. This character couldn't act. He wasn't romantic; he was effeminate. In Nazimova's production of *Camille,* Rudy cried over his lover! Men didn't cry, but the women loved it. With his next film, *The Sheik,* his success reached unprecedented heights. Riding off into the desert on a white steed, carrying a woman against her will to red-hot romance under the moon . . . oh, brother. This movie was so steamy, doctors were called into theaters across the country to care for crowds of fainting fans. Arab designs flooded the day's fashions and interior design, and sales of hair pomade skyrocketed. So did the sales of a new brand of condoms that took the name *Sheiks.* Jazz babies and flappers took to calling their fellas sheiks, and soon it was a household word. Even

Domineering and rumored to be a lesbian, Natacha hurt him personally and professionally. Then she left.

Rodolf Valuntino

At Metro with his 1920 Cord limo.

Webster's dictionary recognized the new meaning: *sheik*—a man supposed to he endowed with an irresistible fascination in the eyes of romantic young women.

Rudy moved to Paramount and continued to score sensationally at the box office. But his career began to falter under the guidance of his second wife, Natacha Rambova, born Winifred O'Shaughnessy, stepdaughter of cosmetic king Richard Hudnut. Guess what? She was also part of Nazimova's group, as her costume designer. Too bad he wasn't paying attention the first time. Natacha and Rudy were married in Mexico in 1922, but there was one problem—his divorce from Acker wasn't final. Back in the States, he was jailed for a short time as a bigamist. Must have seemed like old times. The two remarried in Indiana a year later . . . much to the dismay of Paramount. Rambova was real opposition.

Natacha believed in a special occult power that made her completely infallible in matters of her husband's career. Right, infallible. She begged him not to make *The Sheik.* He fought her on that one, but under her thumb, his image became more and more effeminate, both offscreen and on. Plus she'd make statements like: "A real union is a spiritual one, not one of the flesh." What the hell was that supposed to mean? She was killing this guy's image. She plunged him into debt with independent productions that were never completed and two incredible homes, one of which she never set foot in. And she interfered so often at the studio that Paramount contractually barred her from Rudy's sets. Rudy was torn in half between his work and his wife. Humiliated, Natacha fled to Paris; Rudy followed, but she wouldn't come back. He returned to Hollywood to try to rebuild his crumbling life and career.

A big romance with the hot-blooded Polish star Pola Negri did a lot to restore his romantic image. His screen popularity picked up with a hit, *The Eagle,* but just when he was back on top, he was blind-sided with a stinging editorial in the *Chicago Tribune* entitled "Pink Powder Puff." The writer lashed out when he was confronted by a powder-vending machine in a men's washroom: "It is time for a matriarchy if the male of the species allows such things to persist. Better a rule by masculine women than effeminate men." He wailed that Valentino should have been drowned long ago, "before the next generation of young men discarded razors for depilatories and the old caveman virtues for cosmetics, floppy pants, and slave bracelets." He blamed Rudy, "the beautiful gardener's boy . . . the painted pansy" for the demise of masculinity.

Furious, Valentino responded in manly fashion. "You slur my Italian ancestry; you cast ridicule on my Italian name; you cast doubt upon my manhood. . . . If that son of a bitch thinks I'm a sissy, I'll let him feel my fist against his jaw." The challenge was taken up by Frank O'Neil, boxing expert for the *New York Evening Journal.* Rudy vindicated his honor, beating O'Neil in a few rounds, but the *Tribune* opened the door for attack and American men came rushing through.

Most American men had a hard time with Valentino's extravagances, his fancy way of dressing, his submissive attitude toward the women in his life. He openly referred to Natacha as "The Boss" and was truly a pushover for any determined woman. No wonder men hated him. It was not even close to what they were used to, not the swashbuckling dash of the manly Fairbanks. This was a man who used face cream and hair oil, who wore jewelry and chinchilla-lined coats. Valentino brought a distinctly European flavor that smacked of culture and sophistication. Then their wives and girlfriends turned to goo at the mention of his name and fantasized about the dramatic, steamy sex that Rudy promised to provide. How could they possibly compete with that? They couldn't, so they tried to tear him down.

What was the real story about his wives? What were the whispers of his dalliances during his early career as a dancer and the controversial company he kept in Hollywood, artists and bohemians and the like? Homophobic fear ran rampant in the United States. Journalists who still believed in caveman ethics grunted loudly and beat the ground with clubs. Thousands of men, whose women now found their lovemaking and their ideas about women old-fashioned, knocked Valentino at every opportunity. It positively tortured him.

In '26, a few months after the *Tribune* editorial, Valentino, now thirty-one, was hospitalized with a perforated ulcer. He'd been in pain for some time, but, no sissy, he had refused to see a doctor; now it was too late. Even as he lay dying from blood poisoning on that hot August afternoon, in great pain, he asked his doctors, "Now do I act like a pink powder puff?" His manager moaned that the attacks had blunted his will to live. Crowds gathered outside the hospital while more packed into movie houses for *Son of the Sheik,* one of his greatest successes. As dawn was breaking, his brother moved to close the blinds. Rudy whispered, "Don't pull down the blinds. I feel fine. I want the sunlight to greet me." He lapsed into a coma and died quietly at 12:10 P.M.

No doubt, the guy had an identity crisis—so confident on the screen, so unsure of himself in private. Time and again, he sought out dominant, self-destructive relationships. The right kind of love and support might have helped relieve his doubts. Then again, maybe the mystery would have dissolved and he'd have faded away, last year's fashion. It's all speculation. And it really doesn't matter because his mark had been made. American men would never be the same again. Neither would American women. And perhaps that is just as it was meant to be. After just five short years as a star, Rudolph Valentino is forever remembered as the world's greatest lover. Now that's show biz, baby.

Rudy taught Natacha to make one of his favorite dishes from home.

Spaghetti with Mussels

Chopped garlic is sautéed in olive oil, then chopped tomatoes are added and boiled into a sauce, then mussels are added, still in the shell. Remove and discard any that don't open after 10 or 15 minutes. You may also use clams. Ladle over cooked spaghetti. Add parsley and black pepper to taste.

Mary Astor

eenage Mary Astor was a gorgeous little doll in silent films, innocent and feminine. Under the sheets, it was a different story. Her love life knocked the lid off forbidden sex in the mid-'30s. She had a good start. At eighteen, she learned about sex in the arms of John Barrymore, one of the greatest actors of stage and screen—and more than twice her age. "Mary Astor was so damned beautiful she almost made me faint," he sighed, but in the end, he married someone else. Yeah, she learned, alright. Later, she declared Barrymore was the greatest love of her life. As the nation would soon learn, that made the Great Profile a standout in a crowd.

Her first husband, director Kenneth Hawks, brother of Howard, died in an aerial stunt gone wrong in 1930. Mary found love again in '31 with Dr. Franklyn Thorpe. They had a daughter, Marilyn. The marriage was not made in heaven, but it had plenty of stars. Early in '35, Dr. Thorpe, while looking for cuff links in Mary's undies drawer—yeah, it was like that—received the shock of his life in the form of a powder blue book, a blow-by-blow account of sexual adventure. Mary Astor's diary had been discovered.

As a horrified Dr. Thorpe turned the pages, he discovered that Mary's admiration for the brilliant Broadway and Hollywood playwright George S. Kaufman continued offstage and into the bedroom. Seems the author of *Dinner at Eight, Stage Door,* and *The Man Who Came to Dinner* had a sword even mightier than his pen. "Once George lays down his glasses, he is quite a different man. His powers of recuperation are amazing and we made love all night long . . . we shared our fourth climax at dawn . . . was any woman happier?"

Thorpe sued for divorce. Then he proved he could strike as low a blow as Mary. He declared her an unfit mother and asked for full custody of Marilyn. Now, even today, people look at a woman sideways when her husband demands custody; in 1935, it was practically unheard of. She filed a countersuit and the battle was on.

The judge dismissed the hot diary as hearsay, not evidence. Thorpe didn't get mad, he got even, releasing panting pages to the press who jumped on it like dogs in heat, reprinting long excerpts sprinkled with asterisks. Like Watergate's "expletive deleted" decades later, the public had a ball filling in the blanks. What better way to start a day than debating over morning coffee: "We saw every show in town, had grand fun together and went frequently to 73rd Street where he ****ed the living daylights out of me . . ." or "Ah, desert night with George's body *****ing into mine as we lay naked under the stars."

A sadder but wiser Mary Astor in court.

Four pages of the diary contained Mary's Top Ten. A number of Hollywood's leading men were terrified that their names appeared in the diary—or worse, low on the list.

But the doctor was not without fault. The maid testified Dr. Thorpe had a cozy bed-side manner all his own that included a string of chorus girls, one of whom fought with Thorpe in front of the child—wearing nothing but red toenail polish.

In the end, Mary won custody of her daughter, but at what cost? Would a sex scandal ruin her career, as it had Clara Bow's, just six years earlier? It wasn't the sex that ruined Clara, it was the timing. Mary—wife, mother, adulteress—was much luckier to get caught ****ing toward the end of the depression. Four tough years of poverty, hardship, and you'll-take-it-and-like-it brought people to their senses. Hell, sex was all most of 'em had! Fans not only forgave Mary, they found her more interesting.

The diary scandal set Astor up perfectly for the 1940s, when her on-screen image went from damsel to dame. She was unforgettable in *The Maltese Falcon* in 1941 and won the Best Supporting Actress Oscar that same year for her role as a career musician in *The Great Lie*. On-screen or off, Astor left no doubt that in the war between the sexes, she came fully loaded.

When it comes to cooking, seems Mary was still trying to put one over on us. "It's a really delicious dish," she said, "and your guests will never suspect that it is nothing but glorified round steak. It deserves a permanent place in your menus."

Rouladen or Mock Birds

1	round steak, cut ¼-inch thick
¼	cup flour
1	teaspoon salt
	Sliced bacon
	Sliced Spanish onion
	Bay leaf
	Soup stock

Cut the steak into pieces about the size of the hand, allowing one for each person. Sift the flour with the salt and dip the meat into it. Place on each piece two slices bacon, two slices onion, and a small piece of bay leaf. Roll, tuck in the edges, and tie with a string. Dip again in the flour and fry in good drippings to a deep brown. Cover with boiling stock, cover the pan and cook until tender, at least 1 hour. Remove the strings before serving.

Clara Blandick

If everybody in Hollywood with talent and a strong work ethic got the credit they deserved, you'd know who Clara Blandick was. Thirty-three years in Hollywood, 118 movies, and I'll bet you can't name one . . . well, maybe just one. All those years, and Clara is remembered for one week's work in a little ditty called *The Wizard of Oz*.

Blandick had been on the stage in leading roles for more than twenty years. But it was a hard life on the road. Her marriage in 1911 lasted only one year, and drafty theaters and rooming houses took a toll on her health. Nearly fifty, she settled in Hollywood to work in those new "talking pictures." Her sturdy, Midwestern looks scored her dozens of supporting roles, mostly as a mother. She really delivered the goods as mean old Aunt Polly in *Tom Sawyer* and *Huckleberry Finn*. But after just a few years, Clara seemed doomed to day player stuff, unbilled bits and supporting parts in a number of top productions, including *A Star Is Born*. It wasn't much, but it was a living.

She didn't know when she got a week's work on *The Wizard of Oz* that she'd be appearing in one of the most memorable films of all time. Nobody did. It was nothing special. And the role of Auntie Em was the least special. The MGM casting director lobbied the powers that be for their own brilliant May Robson, but they wouldn't listen. Remember, these are the same know-it-alls who wanted to cut "Over the Rainbow" from the film because it slowed down the story. These mugs considered the role of Auntie Em too minor to cast from their contract players. They claimed they didn't have anyone who fit the part; bad news for Robson, but immortality for Clara Blandick. She is billed last, below Pat Walshe, the head flying monkey. But Auntie Em's salary of $750 a week was not at the bottom of the list. Believe it or not, the film's star, Judy Garland, was low man on the totem pole, under contract at $500 a week. Only Toto got less at $125. Ray Bolger and Jack Haley topped the list at $3,000.

After her week's work as Auntie Em, Blandick went back to tiny, uncredited roles in "A" pictures and good supporting parts in "B" efforts. But with the years came crippling arthritis and failing eyesight. It forced her into retirement in 1950 and eventually forced her hand. At eighty, she was nearly blind and in constant pain. The old gal had had a long run, but the time for her final bow had arrived.

On Palm Sunday, 1962, Clara did her hair, put on her best dress, and went to church. Afterward, in her modest Hollywood apartment, she changed to an elegant blue dressing gown and wrote a farewell note: "I am now about to make the great adventure. I cannot endure this agonizing pain any longer. It is all over my body. Neither can I face impending blindness. I pray the Lord my soul to take. Amen." Then the actress surrounded herself with photos and scrapbooks from her sixty-year career. Though she could barely see them, she knew them all by heart; and her heart was full. After a while, she swallowed a handful of sleeping pills. For insurance, Clara tied a plastic bag over her head. Then she wrapped a gold blanket around her, lay down on the couch, and made it over the rainbow.

This is the way your grandma roasted chicken back in Kansas.

Auntie Em's Roasted Chicken

1	whole chicken, 4 to 7 pounds
	Salt
3	tablespoons melted butter

Position a rack in the center of the oven. Preheat the oven to 400°. Lightly oil a shallow roasting pan or baking sheet. Remove the neck and giblets from the chicken, then rinse and pat dry. Generously rub the body and neck cavities and sprinkle the skin with salt.

Place the chicken in the pan, breast side up. Brush the breast and legs with butter.

Put the chicken in the oven and roast. It's done when the thickest part of the thigh releases clear juices when pricked deeply with a fork. The total roasting time for a 4-pound bird will be 55 to 65 minutes. For larger birds, add 8 minutes for each additional pound.

Remove the chicken to a platter and let stand for 15 minutes. Carve and serve.

Jack's Café served Bugsy Siegel his last supper.

Benjamin "Bugsy" Siegel

His nickname, Bugsy, was for his hair-trigger temper, but better not call him that to his face—Ben or Benjamin, but never Bugsy. As a kid growing up in New York's Hell's Kitchen, his best buddy was Meyer Lansky. These young punks were very enterprising in the neighborhood. Bugsy started with rape, robbery, and murder, then advanced to book-making, bootlegging, smuggling heroin from Mexico, hijacking—all by the age of twenty-one. Eventually Bugs and Lansky formed a little gang of contract killers in New York and Jersey.

At twenty-seven, Siegel was part of an informal cartel that controlled bootlegging across the country. In '33, he decided to visit some of his Hollywood assets. Boyhood chum George Raft provided the perfect entrée. He'd done all right for himself in the movies. Bugsy loved the movies and the stars. He entertained dreams of acting himself, and Raft fixed it so he could have a screen test, but he stunk. He satisfied himself with rubbing elbows. Private encounters with public enemies were dangerous and exciting. Hollywood and the mob were impressed with each other. Siegel was good-looking, personable, and, as long as you didn't make him mad, a swell guy. Raft introduced him to Jean Harlow, Clark Gable, Norma Shearer, Cary Grant, and even a bona fide countess, Dorothy di Frasso—a real cultured tomato. She and the count had some kind of understanding. He was never around, and Dorothy gave the best parties in Hollywood. The countess had her pick of lovers and for a while she picked Bugsy. The pair traveled to Italy, where she introduced him to a whole new way of life: vintage wines, art, custom-tailored suits, high society. Dorothy took a good-lookin' guy and gave him style and sophistication. It fit Bugsy like a glove.

In '35, Siegel moved to L.A. to consolidate mob-controlled gambling in California. Mrs. Siegel stayed home with the children while he looked up his old friend Jean Harlow and squired her to dinner and clubs. Harlow liked him, but she loved his daughters. She begged to be their godmother, and Bugsy thought that was swell. Rumor has it Siegel asked Jean for a favor, too, a lock of her pubic hair. What's a little snip between pals?

The woman who stole Bugsy's heart was not the glamorous Harlow but the petite, gray-eyed beauty Virginia Hill. This Alabama lass drove guys right off their nut. She handled "social affairs" for Lucky Luciano and Frank Costello in New York. In 1941, she set up operations in Hollywood, even landed a few movie roles. When Siegel met her, he didn't know it, but he'd met his match.

Hobnobbing in Hollywood, Bugsy got friendly with Billy Wilkerson, a colorful figure on the social scene. Hell, he created the social scene. In the late '30s and '40s, Wilkerson founded several nightclubs, among them Ciro's and Café Trocadero—both industry Meccas that helped make the Sunset Strip famous while earning Wilkerson the nickname "Father of the Sunset Strip." A ladies' man, he had an eye for female talent, spotting, among others, high schooler Lana Turner in a malt shop. And you could read all about Lana in the *Hollywood Reporter,* a daily motion-picture trade paper he founded in 1930. In 1945, Wilkerson had a new idea—a brilliant plan for a playground in the desert of Las Vegas. He bought some property, but he needed money to develop it. He offered Bugsy a partnership, and Siegel shook on it. Soon after, Siegel "convinced" Wilkerson to sell his share of the dream.

Siegel told Lansky and the boys about "his" vision of a playground for the rich and famous. They liked it and loaned him money to build. Construction on the Flamingo Hotel and Casino began in the spring of 1946. Siegel ran the operation, but he had no hands-on experience in business. The contractors saw an easy mark with deep pockets. He'd order two tons of concrete; they'd deliver one, steal it back at night and redeliver it the next day. Siegel never did catch wise. As the opening on December 26 approached, the hotel wasn't finished and costs spiraled out of control. The boys weren't happy.

To guarantee a sensational opening, Siegel sent cases of liquor to reporters in exchange for good reviews. He hired a fleet of planes to bring celebrities from L.A. The studios had discouraged attendance, but it didn't matter. A big storm grounded the planes. The opening was a disaster. Casino losses the first week were $300,000. Bugsy and Virginia fought and she left—some say with a case full of dough. The boys back east, in for $5 mill, were plenty upset. They wanted to pull the plug on Siegel right there, but Lansky convinced them to give him one more chance.

Siegel promised to get the kinks out for another opening in March. Virginia came back to help, but business did not improve. The boys suspected Bugsy and his girl were skimming off the top. Lansky tried to warn him, but Ben thought he was untouchable. Hill knew better. She urged him to sell and scram to Europe with her, but Bugsy refused to give up his dream. She flew to Paris without him.

June 19, 1947, started as a good day. Siegel was in L.A., staying at Virginia's Beverly Hills home. Her brother, Charlie, and his fiancée, Jeri Mason, who was also Virginia's secretary, were staying there, too. In the morning, Bugsy met with his lawyer, got a haircut, and grabbed lunch with some pals.

It was a warm summer night. Bugsy, Charlie, Jeri, and Al "Smiley" Davenport drove out to the beach for dinner. They got back to the Linden Drive home about twenty minutes after ten o'clock. Charlie and Jeri went upstairs. The boys settled in the living room. Siegel turned on a couple of lamps to read the evening paper. He faced the front window and never even thought about lowering the shades, chatting with Smiley as he flipped through the news of the day. He never saw it coming.

Around 10:45, Smiley heard firecrackers. He looked up to see Bugsy's face covered in blood. The window exploded as bullets sprayed the room and broken glass flew everywhere. Smiley hit the floor. He screamed to Jeri, but she misunderstood and ran downstairs. Smiley screamed again, but she wasn't in danger. The killer hit his intended target and made his getaway. He'd walked right up to the window, just ten feet from Siegel, and fired his army-style carbine at point-blank range. Siegel was shot five times, deader than a mackerel.

Twenty minutes later, two mob associates walked into the Flamingo and informed the manager that the place was under new management. Siegel, forty-one, bet against the house . . . and lost everything.

On the last night of his life, Ben Siegel dined on the Ocean Park pier at Jack's Café. The grilled trout was to die for.

Grilled Trout Fillets with Olive Oil and Lemon

4 servings

1½ to 2 pounds trout fillets at least 1-inch thick, skin on, rinsed and patted dry

1 tablespoon extra-virgin olive oil

Salt and ground black pepper to taste

Lemon wedges

Vinegar

Brush the fillets with the olive oil. Sprinkle with salt and pepper to taste.

Prepare a medium-hot fire. Make sure the rack is clean and place it about 4 inches from the heat.

Place the fillets on the grill, skin side down. Cover, and check after 8 minutes. (If you do not cover the grill, turn very carefully with a wide spatula after no less than 3 minutes.)

Serve immediately with lemon wedges and several drops of vinegar.

Joan Crawford

a Crawford? A movie star like no other: big shoulders, driving ambition, ruthless mother, and image, image, image. The girl was real opposition. She honed it; she owned it—she, Lucille La Sueur, hewed the image of movie star.

Born out of wedlock to a poor family, Joan worked as a servant in a girls school to get an education. She graduated to a chorus line in a Chicago nightclub, which got her to New York . . . which got her to Hollywood, where her ambition and determination to become somebody were her reason to live. Joan worked as a waitress, a salesgirl, and a laundress before dancing her way into an MGM contract and clawing her way to the top. She'd kick it, kiss it, or sleep with it to get what she wanted. And when she got it, buster, what she did with it. *Grand Hotel, Rain, Mildred Pierce, Humoresque.* Few rivaled her for star glamour; yeah, Joan made it, Oscar and all. And she held on. Her legions of fans had long memories. Joan Crawford was a movie star for nearly fifty years.

Joan and the doomed Marie Prevost in *Paid,* 1931.

And with the star came the reputation. The dame was tough as nails. Her temper was legendary, her venomous comments well known, particularly regarding arch rival Bette Davis. There were many, many affairs. Director Vincent Sherman said her sexuality was positively rampant. ". . . a female who went after what she wanted and was masculine in her approach to sex. . . . I had never encountered such female aggressiveness." Her ego seemed insatiable.

Sex was one thing, love was another. Joan never seemed to get the hang of that. After three divorces, she decided she wanted children without the trouble of a husband. Her four adopted (some say "bought") children were barely more than props, paraded out to bow and curtsy and kiss "Mommie Dearest" on cue for the press and the public. Daughter Christina waited until after Joan's death to write a scathing biography chronicling her mother's cruel, manipulative, obsessive behavior. Joan had had a tough childhood. She had no idea what it was like to be a kid . . . or a mother.

But the big surprise is the kinder, gentler Joan, the little-talked-about loyal friend to the down-and-out. Pretty Marie Prevost was full of razzle-dazzle in the early days as a Sennett Bathing Beauty. She and Joan made a couple of pictures together, but as Marie's hips got bigger, her parts got smaller. With sound, they dried up all together. That's when Marie

Mommie Dearest with Christina.

turned to booze in a big way. When authorities found her dead in her bottle-strewn apartment, they also found IOUs to Joan, who'd quietly lent her old pal money until better times returned. And what about Billy Haines? He and Joan starred together in a couple of light romantic comedies at MGM. He was a popular guy on-screen and off, then a tabloid threatened to reveal his homosexuality and MGM forced his retirement. Undaunted, Haines opened an interior design studio on the Sunset Strip, but Hollywood, terrified of guilt by association, stayed away in droves. Not Joan. She hired Billy to redecorate her entire home. When she showed off the gorgeous results, no one cared if Billy Haines slept with goats; they all wanted him. But no one would have gone near him if it

Dishing with a friend.

hadn't been for Joan. She related to the underdog. Not that long ago, she'd been one herself.

In the 1970s, life took an unhappy turn for Joan. She cut her children from her will "for reasons which are well known to them." She was being ousted from the board of Pepsi-Cola—a position she inherited upon the death of her fourth and final husband, Alfred Steele. Offers of work were few. She had no purpose. Her looks were gone. Some say she had cancer. The cruelest blow of all came when Bette Davis was awarded the American Film Institute's Lifetime Achievement Award. That was the final straw. In the weeks before she died, Joan gave away many of her belongings, finding homes for all the things she loved. Her 1976 Christmas card read, "I am so at peace with the world that I'm even having good thoughts about Bette Davis."

There are several theories about what happened that Friday in May 1977. Some say the seventy-three-year-old movie star had been bedridden for weeks. Others, that she was up and making breakfast. She'd made arrangements for her beloved dogs to stay with a close friend while she went out of town for the weekend. But Joan never left town. Instead, on the anniversary of her marriage to Steele, her happiest union, she succumbed to: (a) a heart attack; (b) cancer; or (c) an "accidental" overdose of sleeping pills. Either way, lonely and forgotten, Joan Crawford slipped away to a land where old movie stars never die.

To raise money for the Motion Picture Country home, the last stop for many industry professionals, Joan donated this recipe to the Motion Picture Mother's Cookbook *in 1970. With Joan's love of entertaining, it serves ten.*

Joan's Meat Loaf

2	pounds ground sirloin
1	pound bulk pork sausage
1	pound ground veal
3	raw eggs
1	large Bermuda onion, finely chopped
2	raw green bell peppers, finely chopped
3	tablespoons Lawry's seasoned salt
3	tablespoons Lea & Perrin's Worcestershire sauce
3	teaspoons A-1 Steak Sauce
4	whole hard-boiled eggs
1	cup water

Preheat the oven to 350°. Combine meats, unbeaten eggs, onion, peppers, 1 tablespoon Lawry's salt, 1 tablespoon Lea & Perrin's Worcestershire sauce, and 1 teaspoon A-1. Mix thoroughly. Shape the mixture into an oval loaf form in a large, shallow baking pan. Gently press the hard-boiled eggs into the loaf. Sprinkle with the remaining seasoned salt, Worcestershire sauce, and steak sauce on top of the loaf, as a crust. Pour 1 cup of water in the base of the roasting pan—do not pour over the meat loaf after you have put on the salt and sauces. Bake for 30 minutes. Reduce the oven temperature to 300° and bake for another 30 minutes. Reduce the oven temperature again to 250° and bake for another 45 minutes to 1 hour, basting frequently with the pan juices.

Robert Mitchum

Robert Mitchum was a gorgeous side of beef with terrific shoulders, slim hips, and the kind of sleepy bedroom eyes that drove women crazy. Gals and guys both were drawn to his rugged, straightforward manner. *The Story of G.I. Joe* (1945) earned him an Oscar nomination for Best Supporting Actor. But his tough-talking, indifferent manner in gritty films like *Out of the Past* had fans screaming, "Make mine Mitchum!" He was the very definition of *I don't care.* Nothing bothered Bob Mitchum, or so he thought until August 31, 1948.

That night, Bob and a friend stopped at the Laurel Canyon bungalow of twenty-year-old starlet Lila Leeds. She and her roommate had no sooner asked the guys in than someone lit up a marijuana cigarette and began passing it around. Suddenly, two men burst through the door, guns drawn. Mitchum thought it was a robbery. He was knocked for six to see Lila hand over some joints and pills from her pocket. A cop slapped cuffs on Bob. "I'm ruined," he moaned, "washed up."

Mitchum and Lila Leeds prepare to plead guilty.

Make mine Mitchum!

A swarm of reporters descended on the group at the Hollywood police station. Miss Leeds smiled for all the cameras while poor Bob was left stark naked in shackles, to be questioned by shrinks.

"Do you go to parties often?" they asked. "What do you do?"

Without hesitation, he replied, "Get drunk, follow pretty broads, make a fool of myself, stagger home."

"And what do you do at parties with men?" they asked.

"Talk dirty. Play poker. Get drunk."

"And do you go out with pretty girls?"

"Oh no," replied Bob. "My wife won't let me."

Bob's wife rushed to his side offering love and support. And RKO kingpin Howard Hughes worked behind the scenes to save his star, rushing an unscheduled movie into production so that at the trial, Bob's attorney could plead for probation, claiming his absence would put hundreds of innocent people out of work. A clever plan, but the judge wasn't buying.

To save further notoriety, Mitchum and Lila Leeds pleaded guilty at the trial, receiving sixty days in jail and two years probation. They served fifty, with ten days off for good behavior.

With Mitchum in the slammer, RKO lost no time capitalizing on their star's troubles. They rushed several pictures into release, all of which did well at the box office while garnering good reviews for the thirty-one-year-old Bob. If anything, his one big night at the "reefer resort" only added to his provocative image.

The press had a field day as moralists damned him and liberals hedged. The LAPD announced this as just the beginning of their great Hollywood cleanup.

Miss Leeds soon found she didn't have much to smile about. With the double standard in full effect, her involvement in the episode was fuel for exploitation. She starred in a "B" movie called *Wild Weed,* but little else was offered. During her time behind bars, some of the girls turned her on to the needle, and on the outside poor Lila found herself in hot water again and again. Drunk driving, failed romances, heroin addiction, solicitation, a nervous breakdown; her problems went on and on. Her blossoming career was nipped in the bud that night in the Hollywood Hills.

At an appeal two years later, Mitchum's guilty verdict was dismissed. Rumors flew that nonconformist Bob had been framed to make him more amenable to industry big-wigs. Whatever the case, Hollywood's bad boy never got into trouble again.

The LAPD got their conviction, but the announced "first of many" became the first and only. Seems the big drug bust of 1948 was something of a bust itself . . . unless you were Lila Leeds.

After Mitchum smoked a doobie, he loved to chow down on this dish. And apparently he didn't care how much of which ingredients he used because he didn't give the Motion Picture Mother's Cookbook *any measurements.*

Mitchum's Fettuccine alla Alfredo

Use two pots of unsalted water. Bring the first pot to a boil and add fettuccine egg noodles, stirring slightly to prevent matting. When noodles are boiling rapidly, remove from the heat, drain through a colander, and return the noodles to the second pot that has been brought to a boil.

Prepare a large, warmed mixing bowl by rubbing it with 1 teaspoon olive oil and 1 clove of bruised garlic.

When the fettuccine is nearly transparent (15 or 20 minutes), drain quickly and toss in the bowl with fresh creamery butter, fresh cream, and freshly grated Parmesan cheese. Mix well while still hot and serve topped with grated Romano cheese.

The cheeses should provide sufficient salt for the dish. The DeCecco brand of fettuccine is recommended as it is relatively starch-free, but any hard semolina egg noodle should be suitable if cooked in two waters.

Lana Turner

On a spring day in 1937, Judy Turner ditched typing class at Hollywood High to get a Coke across the street at the Top Hat Malt Shop. (Once and for all, it was not Schwab's Drugstore.) As she sat quietly sipping her drink, a very important man named Billy Wilkerson asked her a very important question: "Sweetheart, how'd you like to be in the movies?" She thought for a moment, then shot back, "I'll have to ask my mother." Mama Turner gave the nod, and a teenage star was born.

Lana Turner's talent in a sweater left guys gasping for air. She started in *Andy Hardy* kids' stuff but soon dazzled audiences in films like *Ziegfeld Girl* and *Johnny Eager.* As a top WWII pinup girl, she inspired many an enlisted man to come back home to Mama. After the war, MGM turned up the heat, transitioning her to full-on glamorous movie star in films like *The Postman Always Rings Twice* and *The Bad and the Beautiful.* By the '50s, she was queen of MGM. Beauty, wealth, legions of adoring fans, and an Oscar nom-

Lana, after the full MGM glamour treatment.

ination for *Peyton Place*—Lana had it all . . . all but true love.

Lana's luck with men was rotten. She was a bad shopper. Fan magazines followed her string of broken romances with Artie Shaw, Frank Sinatra, Howard Hughes, Tyrone Power, Fernando Lamas, and more. By 1957, she'd been married four times; her lifetime total would reach seven. With husband number two, actor Stephen Crane, she had her only child, a daughter, Cheryl. As a mother, Lana was a better bride. It was her world—everyone else just lived in it. She was too busy with her career to notice when husband number four, screen Tarzan Lex Barker, began sexually abusing poor Cheryl. When she found out, she held a gun to the sleeping bastard's head, but she couldn't pull the trigger. Instead, she sent the big ape packing and Cheryl to boarding school. With Cheryl gone, Mama quickly found another lover. Now, she'd had trouble with men in the past, but she didn't know trouble till now.

In 1958, Lana picked a real doozie: smalltime hood and bigtime ladies' man, Johnny Stompanato, a henchman for mobster Mickey Cohen. Good-looking in a smarmy sort of way, and apparently gifted in the sack, he made a good living off lonely, rich women like Lana. So what if he knocked her around a little? She thought it was exciting . . . to a point.

April 4, 1958, Cheryl, fourteen, was home from school, lucky for Lana. Friends say she had been trying to dump the loser for a while, but he was not going quietly. She gave expensive gifts, took him to A-list affairs. She planned to take him to the Academy Awards, but this night she told him he wasn't going there or anywhere with her. He slapped her and told her if she didn't take him he'd ruin her face so she'd never work

Lana, Johnny, and Cheryl one month before his death, March 1958.

March 3, 1958
Lana Turner, daughter Cheryl, &
Johnny Stompanato

again. Cheryl, hearing everything outside the bedroom door, ran downstairs, terrified, and grabbed a kitchen knife. She charged back upstairs. As she burst into the room, Stompanato turned toward her and, somehow, the knife accidentally plunged into his stomach.

When a movie star is involved in a crime, the last person they want to see is a cop. For four decades, the first person they wanted to see was Jerry Geisler, attorney to the stars. He defended Chaplin, Flynn, Mitchum, Bugsy Siegel, even handled one of Marilyn Monroe's divorces. And now Lana. "Get me Geisler" rushed to Bedford Drive. Some say Johnny was still alive and Geisler let him bleed out. The rumor that won't die is that Lana killed Johnny and Geisler convinced her to let Cheryl, a minor, take the fall. One thing's for sure: He made decisions as to how this thing was going down, and Lana and Cheryl

A dazed Cheryl is fingerprinted after stabbing Johnny.

never, ever veered from their story. Geisler accompanied the duo to the Beverly Hills Police Department, where Cheryl, confused and scared stiff, was fingerprinted and booked on suspicion of murder. The next day, the world heard the news. And it was very big news.

Lana and Johnny's lurid love affair exploded across the headlines. Not since Mary Astor's diary had a star's private life been so public. Overnight, the country's take on Turner took a nosedive. Nobody'd ever given much thought to her maternal side, least of all Lana. As a whole, the public felt "Life with Lana" was no place for a young girl. Yes, Cheryl was the real victim here. Many damned Lana, including top columnist Hedda Hopper. "My heart bleeds for Cheryl!" cried Hopper, calling Turner "a hedonist without subtlety . . . so preoccupied with her design for living . . . Cheryl isn't the juvenile delinquent; Lana is." Even the *Hollywood Reporter*—founded by none other than Billy Wilkerson, the man who had discovered the teenage Turner in that malt shop—pointedly wrote that the "town's sympathy is with Steve Crane and his daughter."

The press buildup was pure Hollywood: Stompanato's funeral; Turner's insistence that the hoodlum was an "unwelcome" presence in her life; his brother's announcement that Johnny was stabbed while lying down. The coup de grâce came two days before the inquest when "Lanita's" love letters to her Johnny, filled with burning desires, were plastered across front pages worldwide—a little payback from Mickey Cohen, Stompanato's pal.

Geisler arranged for Cheryl to be excused from the coroner's inquest. That made Lana the star of the show. And what a show. Everything that was important to Lana was on the line: her life, her career, her public image, and oh yeah, her daughter. The morning of the inquest, as hundreds of her fans gathered downtown, Lana's makeup and hair people were giving her the works at her Beverly Hills home. She entered that courtroom "camera ready" for the greatest performance of her life. ABC and CBS jointly filmed the proceedings for television while broadcasting them live on radio. In the hushed, sweltering Los Angeles courtroom, Lana Turner breathlessly explained how her teenage daughter came to murder her gangster boyfriend. It was the stuff dreams were made of.

Only the clicking of cameras could be heard during Turner's anguished sixty-two-minute testimony. Weeping and wringing her hands, she described how Cheryl rushed into the bedroom, knife in hand, after overhearing Stompanato threaten her.

"Everything happened so fast . . . I never saw the knife . . . I thought she had hit him in the stomach with her fist." Sobbing, she told of breathing air "into his semi-open lips . . . my mouth against his." She choked, "He was dying." Oh, brother.

The hearing lasted three hours. The jury returned a verdict in less than twenty minutes: justifiable homicide. Mickey Cohen griped to the press, "It's the first time in my life I've ever seen a dead man convicted of his own murder. So far as that jury was concerned, Johnny just walked too close to that knife."

So go figure. After all the negative publicity, Lana's career was

> "What kind of dish was she? The sixty-cent special—cheap, flashy, strictly poison under the gravy."
> THE NARROW MARGIN, 1952

barely affected. As the '50s neared a close and America settled cheerily into the suburbs, the public created the happy ending they needed to see. Cheryl went to live with her grandmother. The world had one less cheap hood in it. And Lana Turner would carry on, sadder, but wiser. At her next movie, fans cheered her image, shouting, "We're on your side, Lana!" Turner continued to star in films of the '60s and '70s—two of which, *Imitation of Life* and *Madame X,* drew shamelessly on her real-life troubles. P.S. The public loved them.

Even though Lana probably never boiled water without help, she offered up her favorite recipe.

Shrimp Scampi

4 servings

16 medium to large shrimp
¼ stick butter or margarine
¼ cup olive oil
2 cloves crushed garlic
2 tablespoons parsley, ground or fresh
1 tablespoon lemon juice
1 teaspoon salt
¼ teaspoon pepper

Split shrimp and remove the legs, veins, and shell. Leave the tails on. Heat the butter and oil. Add the garlic, parsley, lemon juice, salt, and pepper. Put the sauce on the flesh side of the shrimp and marinate for 1 hour. Place the shrimp in a baking pan flesh side up and broil about 6 inches from the heat for 6 minutes. Serve hot.

John Wayne

Some actors become their roles. With John Wayne, all his roles became him. "John Wayne was a star because he always played John Wayne," Kirk Douglas observed. "Frankly, he wasn't an excellent actor, but good heavens, what a star!"

A huge presence at 6'4", Duke was all shoulders and big arms and blue eyes. His slow walk and talk made him seem like a mountain of a man moving across the screen, usually as a cowboy or in uniform, always the good guy, the one fighting for right and taking no guff from anybody. And as the line blurred between the heroes he played and the man he was, John Wayne became a larger-than-life symbol of the spirit that made this country great. He also became one of the biggest movie stars on God's green earth.

Politically, the guy was a nightmare. He joined in the communist witch-hunt of the '50s and threw full support to the Vietnam War in the '60s. You might disagree, but you had to admit, he was an American.

The Duke's worst performance: Genghis Khan. It wasn't just bad; it was fatal.

That's why it's so ironic. John Wayne, legendary cowboy of the movies, red-blooded, flag-waving, right-wing, Conservative, superhawk American hero, was killed by his own government—contaminated by a nuclear cloud that also rained on the parades of more than half the cast and crew of one of the worst films of the 1950s.

The Conqueror starred John Wayne as Genghis Khan, one of the silliest roles of his entire career. This expensive epic is so bad, it's a camp classic. The movie was shot June through August 1954, near St. George, Utah, 137 miles from the atomic testing range at Yucca Flat, Nevada. The U.S. Government conducted eleven A-bomb tests there. Two were particularly "dirty": "Simon," a 51.5-kiloton blast, and "Harry," a 32.4-kiloton blast. Keep in mind, the Hiroshima blast was only 13 kilotons. A radioactive cloud they named "Dirty Harry" blew directly over the film location and the town of St. George, contaminating the entire area. As if that weren't enough, the unsuspecting film crew brought contaminated dirt from the location back to the studio in Hollywood, so the color of the dirt on the set would match the location. Over time, people who had worked on *The Conqueror* and who lived in St. George started getting sick. Residents and visitors who ate the local meat and produce got sicker faster.

In the early '60s, John Wayne got sick, too. He battled cancer and lost a lung in '63. In '69, he won the Best Actor Oscar for *True Grit.* Cancer returned in the '70s, this time in his stomach. And there was open-heart surgery. He kept working. His last film, *The Shootist,* told the story of a legendary gunfighter who learns he has cancer and tries to die in peace. It was a professional and personal farewell, full of dignity and worthy of such a giant. No matter how you felt about his politics, this was the end of something big. True to his screen persona, the Duke showed courage to the end. In 1979, when he rode off to that final sunset, friends and countrymen remembered him with tremendous affection.

In the years since the movie, more than forty-six members of the cast and crew have died of cancer, including Agnes Moorehead, Susan Hayward, Pedro Armendariz, and director Dick Powell. Of 150 cast and crew members contacted from an original 220, 91 have some form of cancer. Children of Wayne and Hayward who spent time with their parents on the set also contracted various forms of cancer. Residents of St. George have a phenomenally high rate of cancer and thyroid diseases and a decline in SAT scores; 442 victims and their families have filed suit. And a little more irony—St. George is now a popular tourist stop. Utah refers to it as a real "hot spot." God bless America.

Before his stomach was removed in an attempt to beat the cancer that did him in, our cowboy hero loved cooking up this dish.

Cheese Casserole

1	small can evaporated milk
1	tablespoon flour
4	eggs, separated
	Salt and pepper to taste
1	pound Cheddar cheese, coarsely grated
1	pound Jack cheese, coarsely grated
2	cans diced chilies
6	to 8 slices fresh tomatoes or canned stewed tomatoes

Preheat the oven to 325°. Beat the evaporated milk and flour with the egg yolks, and season with salt and pepper. To this mixture, add the stiffly beaten egg whites, folding them in gently. In a well-buttered deep-dish casserole, mix the shredded cheese with the diced chilies. Pour the egg mixture over the cheese and "ooze" it through with a fork. Place the casserole in the oven and bake for 30 minutes. Remove and place the tomatoes on top. Return to the oven and bake for another 30 minutes.

Marilyn Monroe

You don't get to be number one because you're stupid. Marilyn was not stupid, but, as director George Cukor so gracefully put it, "she could be imposed upon . . . and was." Try looking like that and not being "imposed upon" by men. First, it was their idea. Then she discovered she could get what she wanted if men got what they wanted. Modeling jobs, bit parts, the right agent. Give a little, get a little, and when you get a little, run with it, baby. When she was easy, nobody remembered her name. When she got difficult, she was the biggest star in the world. But just because she learned how to work it doesn't mean it didn't hurt. And the pain was always just the least bit visible, something tragic behind the eyes, a quaver in the voice, a sign that told us life and love for Marilyn were never what she hoped for. When she died in August of 1962 at just thirty-six—suicide, accident, or murder—the end result was a broken heart. Was Marilyn truly as fragile as her image? Did she simply lose count of how many pills she'd taken? Or was she mur-

Marilyn hadn't had a decent meal for three days until Tom Kelley took her to Barney's Beanery after she posed for him.

dered because she posed a security risk to important political figures? There are arguments to support all three theories. The bottom line here is that all the evidence has been tampered with. As was the case way back to poor Bill Taylor, Hollywood's oldest unsolved murder, straight through to today, the police are always the last to be called. People were all over the scene removing evidence, planting evidence, arranging the scene so we will never know what happened. All we know for sure is that no matter how she died, Marilyn Monroe died for love. And for the little part in all of us that has been hurt, we hold her close.

That's why the public "forgave" the calendar. May 27, 1949—Marilyn was divorced from Jim Dougherty, behind in her rent and dead broke. She'd had little to eat for three days. A photographer named Tom Kelley had told her anytime she wanted to pose for nudes to call. She'd turned him down a couple of times, but on this day, she called to see if the offer was still open. It was. She went to his studio at 736 North Seward. His wife and sometime assistant, Natalie, was there to help. Tom laid out a sheet of red velvet, put on an Artie Shaw record, and Marilyn took off her clothes. They worked for two hours. He took twenty-four shots. After the shoot, Tom treated Marilyn to lunch. A year or so later, he sold two of the shots.

In '52, as Marilyn was starting to make a name for herself, the calendar came out. Studio execs told her to deny it, but Marilyn refused. "I didn't do anything wrong," she said. Her honesty disarmed the press. She was broke and needed the $50, no excuses. P.S. The calendar made over a million. And the other twenty-two shots? Stolen from Kelley's files.

After the shoot, Tom and Marilyn went for a bowl of chili over at Barney's Beanery, a great little eatery for close to seventy years, frequented by celebrities like Clara Bow, Janis Joplin, and the Barrymores—John and Drew. Here is the famous chili recipe from Barney himself.

Barney's Beanery
8447 Santa Monica Blvd.
Hollywood 46, California

Dear Sir:
    Sorry the recipe you requested is a bit tardy; but we have had so many requests it has taken some time to get them all out.
    My recipe calls for
                2 pounds ground meat (chili grind)
    Braise this meat in heavy pot or pan with 1/3 pound suet grease (or bacon drippings or other grease or compound that is handy).
                    3 to 4 cups hot water
    Then boil 45 minutes (add hot water as needed).
    When cooked add
                2 level teaspoons chili powder
            2 level teaspoons paprika
        2 level teaspoons ground cumin (cuminos)
        1 to 2 level teaspoons ground oregano
    2 Jap chilis (or small red hots), broken very finely
    Salt to taste. Stir thoroughly.
    Keep separate from beans until you are ready to serve it. When cold will keep for several days under refrigeration.
    Dish up the chili with the beans in proportion for the strength desired. Rather hot would be about 50-50.
    A simple bean recipe—
    Beans, chopped onion, canned tomatoes, salt, and pepper. Use your favorite beans—pink, pinto, or kidney.
    Hope you enjoy the chili and beans as much as I did making them for you.

    Good luck,
    Barney Anthony
    Barney's Beanery

Around the same time, March of '52, Yankee slugger Joe DiMaggio started bugging his pal David March to set him up with Marilyn. Marilyn didn't want to go. She didn't like baseball or baseball players. Even though Joe was a national hero, she didn't follow the game and didn't know who he was. But, when Joe came to town to play a charity game, she finally agreed to meet him at the Villa Nova restaurant on the Strip, provided March and a date would also be there. The dinner was for 6:30 on a Saturday night. Marilyn was shooting *Monkey Business* and arrived two hours late. Very little was said, but Marilyn was pleasantly surprised.

"I had thought I was going to meet a loud, sporty fellow. Instead, I found myself smiling at a reserved gentleman in a gray suit, with a gray tie and a sprinkle of gray in his hair. There were a few blue polka dots in his tie. If I hadn't been told he was some sort of ballplayer, I would have guessed he was either a steel magnate or a congressman."

All night, men came over to the table, something she was used to. But this night, they didn't come to talk to her. Mickey Rooney barely noticed her. They wanted to talk to Joe, to shake his hand, to be near him. Marilyn had never seen a guy like this before. She wanted to know more. It was the start of a great romance. And though the marriage lasted less than a year, the love never died. Joltin' Joe and Marilyn could not find a way to happily blend their

Marilyn and Joltin' Joe were set up—on a blind date.

public and private lives, but it was never about not loving each other anymore. Joe was always there for her, even to bury her. He never remarried, and he sent roses to her grave twice a week for more than thirty years. Oh yeah, it was love. And it all started that night at the Villa Nova. Hey waiter, I'll have what they're having!

That magic meal began with anchovies on pimiento, followed by spaghetti al dente and veal scaloppine.

Scaloppine of Veal

1	pound veal scaloppine slices (8 to 12), cut a little more than ¼-inch thick and pounded to slightly less than ¼-inch thick

Salt and ground black
pepper to taste
½ cup all-purpose flour
1 tablespoon olive oil
1 tablespoon unsalted butter

Preheat the oven to 180°. Season the meat with salt and ground black pepper to taste. Place the flour in a shallow dish, and dredge the scaloppine through it. Shake off the excess.

In a large skillet heat the olive oil and butter over high heat. Cook the scaloppine in batches, being careful not to crowd the pan. Brown quickly, 30 to 60 seconds each side. Remove to an ovenproof platter and keep warm in the oven. Repeat, adding more oil and butter to the pan as needed, until all the scaloppine is cooked. Season with salt and ground black pepper to taste. Serve immediately.

Marilyn kept DiMaggio waiting here for two hours. (P.S. It was worth the wait.)

Frank Sinatra

Frankie, the Leader of the Rat Pack, the Boss, Francis to the boys in Chicago. You know who, Frank Sinatra, that skinny kid from Hoboken with the big "vocce."

In the early days, his manager had Frank's suits loosely sewn so when excited bobby-soxers pulled at them, they came off. Oh yeah, Frankie in his boxers was big news back then. Frank never dreamed how big he'd get—the biggest—or maybe he did. Whatever, Frank Sinatra dominated the entertainment industry for more than fifty years, while setting the bar for cool. The cat was smooth—those baby blues, the hat, the clothes, the great nonchalance, but always the top cat, in control. Everybody played by Frank's rules—or they didn't play. Chicks dug him. Men envied him. And everybody respected him—or else. The public saw living proof of his violent mood swings. He did stuff to photographers that makes Sean Penn look like a cream puff. Yet he was also the guy behind countless charitable acts fans didn't see. When the papers reported that Bela Lugosi was destitute and in drug rehab, Frank paid Dracula's bills to thank him for all the good years. Same with Lee J. Cobb. The actor named names to Joe McCarthy at the HUAC trials, so when he fell on hard times, he had few friends left in Hollywood. Frank was at the top of a very short list. When they had worked together years earlier, Cobb had helped Frank with the work. Frank never forgot a favor. Of course, he never forgot a fight, either.

Then there were his women—not his wives, his women. Frank, the Rat Pack, and "the boys" preferred hookers . . . no muss, no fuss. "(They) had deep respect for hookers and treated them with gallantry," said George Jacobs, Sinatra's valet from 1953 to 1968. Frank often told George he preferred "an honest hooker to a conniving starlet." In return, the girls got the high life: travel, gifts, money. When Frank took a shine to a particular girl, say, a cute little Irish number named Judy Campbell, he passed her to his special friends, ". . . like a hot tip on a new restaurant," said Jacobs. That's how Judy ended up in bed with Frank, Chicago mob boss Sam Giancana, and President John F. Kennedy. Baby, that's some pillow talk.

But even the great one could make a mistake. Take the night of November 5, 1954. Frank was dining in Hollywood at Patsy D'Amore's Villa Capri with Joltin' Joe DiMaggio. The two had a lot in common besides their Italian heritage. They understood each other: two poor guys from the neighborhood who become the idol of millions, both hot-tempered and both whipped by a woman, Frank by Ava Gardner and Joe by Marilyn Monroe. Their jealousies almost killed them both and pushed their women away.

Marilyn filed for divorce and Joe flipped. The thought of her with another man sent him over the moon. So, as a favor, Frank had her tailed. That's how they got the word at the Villa Capri that she was holed up with a guy in an apartment. Frank, Joe, and some of the boys charged over there. The building's landlady later testified she saw Frank and Joe arguing in the street about 11:15. Frank tried to calm Joe, but he wasn't buying. He ordered the boys to break down the apartment door. The whole building heard the ruckus. Sinatra and DiMaggio charged in, flashbulbs popping, shouting, but nobody shouted louder than poor Florence Kotz, the fifty-year-old woman who'd been asleep inside. Marilyn, dining with friends a few doors down, made a quick getaway. So did the boys, almost.

The cops—always willing to help a pal—wrote up the incident as an attempted burglary. Flo sued for twenty grand, but settled for $7,500 and the whole thing was hushed up until *Confidential* magazine wrote an exposé two years later on the "Wrong-Door Raid." The sleazy tabloid claimed the two palookas expected to catch Marilyn in the arms of a lesbian lover. A committee of the California State Senate wanted to know how yellow rags like *Confidential* got those stories leaked to them in the first place and asked Frank and his detective to testify. They also asked Joe, but he sent his regrets.

At the hearing, Frank testified he drove Joe there and waited in the car till he returned. The landlady contradicted him, saying Frank and Joe stood back while "the boys" broke down Kotz's door, then burst into the apartment. With so many discrepancies, the judged expanded the investigation. The headlines lasted for months. Frank narrowly escaped perjury charges because it had been too dark for the landlady to be certain of their identities. He denied guilt and the case was dropped.

> *"I didn't squawk about the steak, dear. I merely said I didn't see the horse that used to be tethered outside here."*
> NEVER GIVE A SUCKER AN EVEN BREAK, 1941

DiMaggio never spoke to Sinatra again. He believed Frank set the whole thing up to make him look like a jerk, a point driven home when Sinatra started dating Marilyn. But when Frank passed her to his friends, like he did with his hookers, he became Joe's mortal enemy. "Marilyn was Mr. S's celebrity version of Judy (Campbell)," George Jacobs explains. "He brokered assignations not only between her and JFK, but also Sam Giancana and fellow gangster Johnny Rosselli." The weekend before she died, Frankie made a date for her with Giancana at the Cal-Neva Lodge. The late Sam Melville, star of TV's *The Rookies,* was a driver for the Lake Tahoe casino back in '62. "I was a kid and I couldn't believe she was in my car. I kept staring at her in my rearview mirror. She didn't talk, didn't even smile. She seemed so sad. A week later, she was dead." The whole world buzzed with the shocking news, but not at the lodge. Sam said the subject was taboo.

Joe barred Frank and all his buddies from her funeral, saying, "It was Hollywood that destroyed her—she was a victim of her friends." If Frank cared, it didn't show.

And if he mourned, he drowned his grief the Italian way—in pasta sauce. Mangia.

Sinatra's Quick Italian Tomato Sauce

First, you start with some olive oil and some garlic, four whole cloves. You heat the oil and add the garlic. Puncture the garlic with an ordinary fork so it exudes the flavor. When the garlic turns tan, turn off the oil and throw it out. Save the oil.

Next you take two whole cans of the Italian plum tomatoes. Place them in the blender and count to a slow four. Put the tomatoes into a large saucepan. Add some basil, salt, pepper, oregano, and the oil. Bring the sauce to a boil. Skim the oil that rises to the top. Dip a piece of bread in the sauce testing to see when the sauce is finished. At the end you might want to add some fresh parsley. And there you have it—a good pasta sauce.

Sal Mineo

Susan met Sal Mineo in 1965. She was fresh out of high school, and he was a movie star. They dated; she fell head over heels. "It was the '60s, and we were crazy and everybody was sleeping with everybody. It was the summer of love, and everybody in Los Angeles was getting naked and having a really great time. Being that age, we could afford to do that then—or so we thought." They lived together for years.

"Then" was the beginning of the end for Sal. At sixteen, he had received an Oscar nomination for his 1955 portrayal of Plato in one of the most powerful teen movies ever made, *Rebel Without a Cause.* Sal's desperate image spoke to troubled kids around the world. He became a teen hero. Fan magazines devoted issue after issue to him. He was mobbed in public. He won an Emmy and another Oscar nomination for the role of Dov Landau in *Exodus* in 1960. And with that, his career peaked. The times, they were a-changin'. The '50s punk image was out. The progressive '60s had arrived, ushering in a

Sal was a talented drummer before starring in *The Gene Krupa Story* (1959).

The trip from the Bronx to Hollywood turned a dark corner.

new peace-and-love generation that no longer related to Mineo's tough, street image. Job offers were suddenly few and far between.

Things got worse. "He got hit with a lot of back taxes because his business manager kind of took him for a ride," Susan added. "He said something about (losing) $100,000, and in those days that was a fortune, devastating."

"It didn't matter to the locals that Sal wasn't working as much; he was an icon," recounts Jon Provost, who played Timmy on the *Lassie* television show. Jon hung out with Mineo, listening to music, checking out the clubs on the Sunset Strip. "When Sal Mineo walked into the Whisky, the crowd parted like the Red Sea." How surreal—a has-been by day and a teen idol at night.

The tough guy image was career suicide.

"We had a lot of laughs," Susan fondly recalls. "He was very funny, had a great sense of humor, very witty, very bright, but there was the dark side."

"Black leather jacket, black jeans, Sal always wore black," adds Provost. "Everything Sal had was black. He drove a black-on-black Cadillac. Even the exterior of his house was black. Inside, the furniture was dark and heavy or black leather. Thick drapes were always drawn, blocking out the sun. He kept a black Harley in the living room. Smoke from cigarettes and pot hung in the air in thick clouds. It was a trip."

As his power, fame, and fortune dwindled, Sal grew darker, more intense. He stubbornly refused to change with the times, fighting to control everything around him. Eventually, Susan and Jon had to move on or be dragged under. Hollywood moved on, too. Sal remained in his dark kingdom, immersed in a gay lifestyle. He made *Escape From the Planet of the Apes* in '71. It would be his last film.

In '76, Sal was still trying for a comeback. He hoped a play would draw some attention. He made the headlines, but not the way he expected. On February 12, as he returned from rehearsal to his West Hollywood apartment, neighbors heard his terrified screams. They found him lying on the concrete, his chest covered in blood. Sal had been stabbed repeatedly during a fierce struggle and, despite their efforts to save him, he died as the paramedics were arriving. The thirty-seven-year-old was a random target, a "thrill kill."

Two years later, Lionel Ray Williams, serving time for forgery, bragged to his cellmate about murdering Sal Mineo. The cellmate squealed, and Williams got fifty-one years to life.

When Susan heard of Sal's murder, she was sad, but not surprised. "I really think in many, many ways you create your own reality and you draw in the energy, and he died a very tragic and horrible death."

Poor Sal. When the lights went out for him in Hollywood, he couldn't find his way out of the dark.

When asked about Sal's favorite dish, Susan didn't hesitate. "Linguine with clams. In fact, he taught me how to make it for him." Sal served this with French garlic bread to soak up the sauce. Susan adds, "Under no circumstances should you kiss anyone who did not eat dinner with you!"

Linguine with Clams à la Sal

Linguine
Fresh garlic, minced
Butter
Canned or bottled clams
Parsley, chopped
Salt and pepper to taste

Make the linguine. Mince the fresh garlic and sauté it in butter. Add the clams and a splash of the juice they came in, and stir lightly until sautéed. Pour over the linguine. Add the chopped parsley and salt and pepper to taste.

Sharon Tate

Sharon Tate loved El Coyote Restaurant. She went often, including the night she died. "I had waited on her a lot," says Estella Collier. "She was my customer . . . such a beautiful person, so kind, always smiling."

Sharon, a doe-eyed daughter of an army intelligence officer, grew up all over the United States and abroad. When she hit her twenties, she moved to Hollywood to be an actress, and she was doing all right. In 1966, she was cast in Roman Polanski's film *The Fearless Vampire Killers.* "I didn't believe people like that existed," Polanski later wrote about her. "She was beautiful, without phoniness . . . fantastic . . . an angel. . . ." They fell in love and were married two years later. In 1969, she was twenty-six and expecting their first child, a boy they planned to name Paul.

In 1969, Estella was forty-eight. She'd already been waitressing at El Coyote for twenty-seven years. The joint was jumping back then. "I was so busy because I had so many customers that would ask for my services. Every room filled with people . . . so many celebrities . . . I can name a few . . . a very famous actress, Loretta Young, I waited on her many times. Kim Novak was one of my best customers. Prince Ranier. . . ."

"Loafing" at the market.

The night of August 8, 1969, Sharon came in with three friends, Jay Sebring, Abigail Folger, and Wojtek Frykowski. Roman was in London shooting a film. The reservations were for 8:00 P.M. under Jay's name, but they were forty-five minutes late and the place was packed. Their table had been given away. The manager worked hard to find them another one and finally seated them in a back booth at 9:00. Sharon, eight months pregnant, had trouble squeezing in. Everyone laughed about it. It was a happy evening spent with friends.

"I did not wait on them that night," Estella remembers clearly. "I had a big party and it was late at night. I used to wait on her all the time, but not during a party." Sharon got up from her table. She knew the people at the table Estella was working and felt comfortable going over. It was that kind of place. "She came up to my table because they were friends of hers. She came over to give me a hug. She was a very, very lovable person.

"She spoke of her excitement for the baby and I congratulated her, of course. I hadn't seen her for a while, maybe because she was pregnant. She was so big then, almost ready to deliver. She was pretty big for the first child; usually the first child, you don't get that big. I had six children of my own so I knew. I felt very motherly toward her."

Sharon and her friends finished their dinner at 9:45 and headed back home. Abigail,

Unlike today's "enhanced" starlets, Sharon was 100 percent natural—and just as beautiful inside as out.

the Folger coffee heiress, and boyfriend Wojtek, Roman's friend, were staying with Sharon. Sebring had been Sharon's fiancée. Now the premier men's hairstylist was a good friend to both Polanskis. He lived just a half mile or so up the canyon. He went in to hang out for a little while. Within hours, all four lay in a bloody heap, murdered, along with Steven Parent, by deranged members of the Manson "family" in one of the most horrifying slayings in American history . . . a night few want to remember, but nobody has ever been able to forget.

Tex Watson, Patricia Krenwinkel, and Susan Atkins were young runaways who'd found Charles Manson, a small, psychotic man with icy, penetrating eyes. They all lived together with other members of his "family" at an abandoned movie ranch out in the desert where they indulged in group sex, lots of LSD, and daily sermons from their leader.

He believed the Beatles were speaking to him through their music, urging him to ignite a race

war. He had chosen the Polanski house because he'd been there once to play his music for an unimpressed producer. He instructed his little band of killers to murder everyone in the house and to make it "as gruesome as possible."

Steve Parent was pulling down the driveway on his way out when they arrived. A young student, he'd come by to purchase a clock radio from the caretaker. They shot him first. Then they entered the house and the bloodbath began. One by one, the four were killed: shot, beaten, stabbed dozens and dozens of times. They saved Sharon for last and laughed as she begged for the life of her child. Watson later said he remembered how beautiful she was as she sobbed and called for her mother. He stabbed her sixteen times.

"The next morning . . . oh, you have no idea; I cried, I felt so awful. It was the most horrible thing . . . I couldn't believe that had happened to her and all those people. For me, it was just horrible," Estella choked. She was not alone. Never mind that some of the victims were rich and famous, forget that this was Beverly Hills. The absolute savagery of the crimes was beyond anything the world had seen. And the shock and horror of it do not dim with the passing of time.

"I loved her and I still love her even though she's not here, and I'll always love her because of her kindness, her sweetness. You don't find that very often. . . . People are nice and everything, but Sharon was a very special person. I miss her everyday."

El Coyote opened in the early 1930s, and the gringo Mexican hangout has never lacked for patrons—tourists, locals, celebrities—everybody went to El Coyote. Seventy years later, they still go. Now famous as the scene of Sharon's last supper, fans regularly ask for the back booth, especially on the anniversary of her death. Many a margarita is lifted to her memory on that day. But until now, what Sharon ordered has never been revealed. Estella didn't have to serve her that night to know. Sharon ordered only one thing. "She always ordered enchiladas; she loved the enchiladas . . . just cheese; she never ordered meat."

Cheese Enchiladas

½   pound Longhorn cheese, mild
½   pound Jack cheese

1	small onion, chopped
1	tablespoon flour
1	small can tomato sauce
1	can water
	Chili powder, salt, pepper, and other seasonings to taste
12	tortillas

Preheat the oven to 350°. Grate the cheeses and mix together. Fry the onion in oil until golden, and add the flour, tomato sauce, and water. Season to taste with chili powder, salt, pepper, and whatever seasonings you prefer.

Dip the tortillas in the sauce, spread with cheese, and roll. Use the leftover cheese and sauce on top. Bake until hot and bubbly.

Liberace

In the early 1980s, the country was in the dark about AIDS. The disease was just beginning to make an impact—on the coasts, in the arts. America still thought of it as the "gay plague." Rock Hudson changed that in 1985. The macho leading man had been around a long time, more than thirty years. All that time, he'd kept his fans in the dark about his sexual preference. Diagnosed with AIDS in 1984, he told the public he had liver cancer. Finally, in July 1985, he came clean. It was a double whammy: Rock Hudson was gay and he had AIDS. The one-two punch hit hard. Anybody can get this disease. And, if Rock Hudson was gay, who else might be?

Liberace lived his motto: "Without the show, there is no business." Mr. Showmanship made playing the piano a three-ring circus. He started with a grand piano and a candelabrum. Young Lee, as he was called, was classically trained, but he paid the bills playing in movie theaters and speakeasies. Good-looking, charming in a gooey sort of way, he entertained audiences playing popular tunes in a classical style. It was fun and the guy could play. And play he did: in nightclubs, on the radio, on television, and in film. People who thought they hated classical music liked Liberace. And the women? They were mad about the boy.

Hollywood came calling in 1950. Movies came first, but Liberace found his place on the small screen. *The Liberace Show* debuted as a summertime replacement and grew to become one of the most popular shows on the air, seen in twenty countries. As the times changed, Liberace added flamboyant costumes, sequined hot pants, and a full-length ermine cape. He drove onstage in a Rolls-Royce or flew in on hidden wires. When asked how he could play the piano while wearing so many rings, he replied, "Very well, thank you." Funny guy. Middle-class, middle-American women went wild.

America of the '50s and '60s looked at this man in sequins and furs and did not see a gay man. Homosexuality was an illness, something in the shadows; certainly no one we actually knew was gay. To fend off rumors, Liberace announced his engagement to a young woman named Jeanne Rio. They never tied the knot, but it stopped the gossip for a while. Rock Hudson felt the same pressure and married his secretary in 1957; the sham lasted a year. In '59, Liberace successfully sued a London newspaper for calling him gay. He denied it in court, testifying that homosexuality was an "abomination."

One of the highest-paid entertainers of 1969, Lee's panache and people-pleasing talent earned him Best Dressed Entertainer, Entertainer of the Year, two Emmy Awards, six

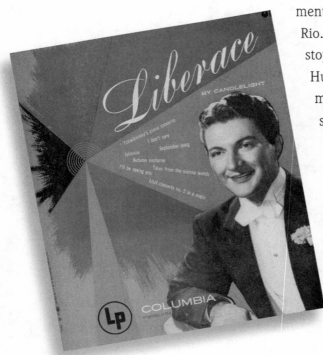

Controversy surrounded the showman's
death . . . enough to hold up his funeral.

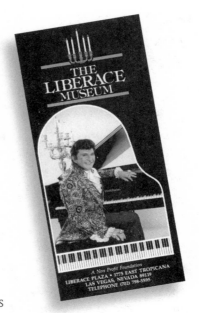

gold albums, and two stars on the Hollywood Walk
of Fame.

Still the press hammered at him, hinting that his
succession of young male chauffeurs drove more than
his cars. The denials became more difficult in '82
when a live-in chauffeur publicly sued Liberace for tin-
kling with his ivories. Still, he continued to deny his
homosexuality, and at the end, his killer.

A lifetime chain smoker, Lee suffered from heart disease and emphysema. His last performance was at Radio
City Music Hall on November 2, 1986. Two months later, he was hospitalized with what
his camp called anemia. Seems the entertainer had eaten nothing but watermelon for a
couple of months, and he needed a doctor to tell him watermelon had no protein. His
manager said Liberace needed six or eight months' rest. He was dead in two weeks. A
funeral was hastily planned.

Then the press broke the story. Liberace had died from AIDS. His manager threatened to sue. The media circus that had surrounded Rock Hudson's final days now swirled
around Liberace. The coroner stepped in to investigate the cause of death. Records dis-
closed that Liberace had been diagnosed with AIDS eight months before his death. The
media had finally gotten their man. And little blue-haired old ladies around the country
turned to each other in shock and amazement to ask, "You mean . . . Liberace was gay?!"

According to his cook, Liberace's last meal was Cream of Wheat cereal with half and half, sprinkled with brown sugar. In healthier days, he shared these recipes with the Motion Picture Mothers. Remember, you are what you eat!

Ham Loaf

2	pounds ground pork
1	pound ground cured ham
1	cup breadcrumbs
½	cup milk
3	tablespoons cream of tomato soup
1	teaspoon paprika
½	teaspoon salt
1	onion

Mix all ingredients and shape into loaf in a baking dish, covering with thinly sliced onions. Bake in a moderate oven for 90 minutes. Baste with hot water.

Mustard Sauce

½	cup tomato soup (undiluted)
½	cup prepared salad mustard
½	cup vinegar
½	cup sugar
½	cup margarine
3	egg yolks, beaten

In a double boiler combine all of the ingredients and cook until thick. Serve with ham loaf.

Natalie Wood

Natalie Wood told loads of people her worst fear was to drown in dark water. Sometimes you can be so afraid of something, you make it happen. All we know for sure is Natalie Wood ended up in the drink, but nobody really knows why.

Thanksgiving weekend 1981 ended with a thud. Natalie Wood, a glamorous, gorgeous movie star, died a cold and lonely death in the water off Catalina Island. That kind of thing didn't happen to a movie star. Especially one like Natalie. Her life was charmed. As the news hit fans returning from their holiday weekend, her life flashed before our eyes. A star at seven, she costarred with James Dean, dated Elvis, married Robert Wagner—twice. The first time ended badly, but they found their way back. The fairy tale had a happy ending, and Hollywood's happiest couple remarried aboard a yacht in the Pacific in '72. We'd been watching Natalie Wood for thirty-five years and suddenly, when it counted, no one was watching. We looked away for a moment and she was gone.

Natalie, nineteen, prepares to marry RJ in 1957.

November 1981: Natalie was filming *Brainstorm* with Christopher Walken. There'd been some rumors about the two stars . . . enough to make Walken's wife fly in for a while. But she wasn't around on Thanksgiving weekend. So Natalie invited Chris to spend the holiday aboard her fifty-five-foot cabin cruiser with husband RJ and two other friends. The weather was dark and gloomy, and the other two canceled, leaving just Walken. If he'd canceled, the Wagners probably would have stayed home.

The trio sailed at noon on Friday with skipper Dennis Davern. Davern had been with the Wagners for six years. You get to know people after six years on a ship every weekend. Dennis became a friend, a friend who worked for them. He partied with their famous friends, drank with them, traded pills with Natalie (he swapped Quaaludes for Valium). He loved working for them. No kidding.

The seas were rough. Landlubber Walken felt sick right away and went to his cabin. They anchored off Catalina Island, twenty-two miles from the Southern California coast, around 5:00 P.M., and he and the Wagners went ashore in their motorized dinghy, the *Valiant*. They shopped, had drinks, and returned to the yacht for dinner, but Walken still didn't feel well and retired. Davern said there was tension between the Wagners. They started in on each other and it got pretty heated.

The fishbowl existence killed their marriage the first time around.

Natalie abandoned ship. She grabbed Dennis, hopped in the dinghy, and went ashore. They stayed at the Pavillion Lodge, drinking and talking all night.

Davern said that the next morning, Natalie was still teed-off at RJ and thought about leaving him there and going home, but she felt responsible for Walken. She returned to the *Splendour* in the morning as if nothing had happened and made huevos rancheros for everybody.

The seas were "grumpy"; even Natalie took seasickness pills. A waitress at Doug's Harbor Reef and Saloon says RJ and Dennis got there first; Dennis recently said Chris and Natalie preceded them and were well in their cups by the time they arrived in the late afternoon. The four decided to have an early dinner. Natalie didn't like the wine list so Dennis and Walken went back to the yacht for some.

At dinner, the waitress thought Natalie's mood was like the weather—dark. She complained; the swordfish wasn't fresh; there was too much light on the table. Davern said she poured it on thick with Walken, flirting and laughing. The foursome put away two bottles of wine and two bottles of champagne; one man had daiquiris. Natalie stumbled a little on the way out. RJ seemed irritated with her.

Wagner told the cops he and Walken had gotten into a political debate at dinner. They kept it up back on the ship. Dennis went to bed and, after a while, Natalie did, too. The guys kept at it another hour before RJ went to check on her; that's when he discovered she was missing. After Natalie's body was found, dressed in a nightgown, it dawned on him what must have happened. He believed the *Valiant* was slapping against the boat, keeping her awake, so she went on deck to untie it and move it, but she slipped, hit her head, and fell into the water.

Davern told the same story at the time, but over the last twenty years, he's "de-sanitized" it. In 2000, he told writer Sam Kashner that after dinner, back on board the *Splendour,* the wine was flowing. Natalie flirted, Walken lapped it up. Suddenly RJ smashed a bottle on the table and called Walken out. Chris got up right away and left. So did Natalie. RJ followed her and, says Davern, they had the biggest fight he'd ever heard, throwing things, screaming, ferocious. Next he heard the dinghy being untied, then there was silence. After some time, Wagner, "tousled, sweating profusely," returned to the bridge about 11:30 and drank another bottle of wine with Davern. At 1:30 RJ went to check on his wife. He came back and told Davern she wasn't in her cabin. Davern looked all over the ship, then saw that the *Valiant* was gone. If she had wanted to sleep onshore, she'd have asked him to take her. It was pitch black, not even stars. He wanted to turn on the floodlights, to fire up the engines and look for her, but he says RJ didn't want to alert the other ships.

Eventually, Wagner called the harbor patrol. They sent three boats out. At 3:25, the Coast Guard joined the search and with dawn's light, a sheriff's helicopter began making passes over the cove. At 7:45, the copter circled over Blue Canyon's Point and a patrol boat raced to the spot. There, they found her body floating face-down just below the water's surface, a mile and a half from the *Splendour.* The *Valiant* was 200 yards away, gears in neutral, key in the "off" position; she never boarded it.

Police and Coroner Thomas Noguchi agreed: Natalie, dressed in a flannel night-gown, down jacket, and wool socks, fell off the swim step while trying to board the dinghy. She wasn't moving it; she was get-ting into it. She untied it, then slipped, hit her cheek, maybe got knocked out. Then she fell into the cold water, a considerable shock, especially after a blow to the head. She clung to the dinghy, trying to hoist herself up,

For moviegoers, it was love at first sight.

never thinking to remove the heavy down jacket. She drifted more than an hour. Someone heard a woman calling for help around midnight. "It went on about forty min-utes. I didn't help because I heard another voice answer, 'Take it easy. We'll be over to get you.'" But no one did help. Finally, overcome by exhaustion and hypothermia, Natalie Wood drowned.

The coroner immediately mentioned some sort of argument on board. People have speculated about that ever since. One tabloid had Wagner and Walken duking it out on deck. One ducked, the other hit Natalie and sent her into the water. And what, the three men didn't notice she fell in? They all stood and watched? There is no way anybody on that yacht knew Natalie was in the water. This was not murder or even manslaughter. Walken feels that "people who are convinced there is something more to it will never be satisfied; there is nothing more to it. It was an accident." Davern implies something darker, saying he knows how Natalie got in the water, but he can't find a publishing house. Wagner has never changed his story. He said there was a heated discussion. Everyone seems to agree there was a lot of drinking and an argument. Why did Natalie try to take the dinghy on dark waters all alone? What was she trying to get away from? There's your answer: a lot of drinking and an argument . . . a stupid, meaningless argument that brought the life of one of the world's biggest movie stars to a haunting end.

Natalie drank Pouilly-Fuissé with her swordfish.

Grilled Swordfish

4 servings

Prepare a medium-hot charcoal fire or preheat a gas grill or the broiler. Make sure the grill rack is clean and place it about 4 inches from the heat on a grill, or 2 to 3 inches from the broiler heat.

1½ to 2	pounds fish steaks (2 large or 4 small), at least 1-inch thick, rinsed and patted dry
1	tablespoon extra-virgin olive oil
	Salt and ground black pepper to taste
	Lemon wedges
	Vinegar

Brush the fish steaks with olive oil. Season with salt and pepper to taste. Place them on the grill or under the broiler. Grill or broil until browned, 3 to 6 minutes; turn and grill the other side until browned, 3 to 5 minutes more. Remove them from the grill just before the interior is opaque. They continue to cook off the heat.

Serve immediately with lemon wedges and several drops of vinegar.

Nicole Brown Simpson

Nicole Brown was eighteen years old and working as a waitress in a Beverly Hills night-club when she met O.J. Simpson, then thirty and married with a family. He was considered by some to have been the greatest running back in American football history and had a lucrative career in Hollywood.

Simpson was possessive and obsessive, and Nicole was oh so willing to please. She moved in with him, made her breasts larger, tried to dress the way he wanted, tried to look good for him. They married in 1985 and had two kids. He berated her for gaining weight during the pregnancies. He smacked her around pretty good. He cheated on her. She could never please him. Eventually, she took the kids and left. They divorced in 1992 but, as just about everyone knows by now, that wasn't the end. They were all tied up in each other. He spied on her; even stalked her. He swore he'd change, pleaded with her to come back. And she did. She even moved back in with him in January of '94, but she called it quits again in May. He just couldn't stand it. He was one of those "if I can't have her . . ." types. He hit her. She called 911. Their breakup was terrible. She feared for her safety. It was an all too typical case of domestic violence with a tragic, but predictable, ending: She died a violent death. He said he didn't do it. But this time, the whole world was watching.

Sunday, June 12, 1994—O.J., Nicole, and her family went to their daughter's school recital in Brentwood. O.J. made a scene and left. After the recital, about 6:30, the Browns dined with Nicole and the kids, just six and nine, at Mezzaluna restaurant. For dessert, they strolled to Ben and Jerry's for chocolate chip cookie dough ice cream, then headed home. At the Brown home, Nicole's mother discovered she had lost her glasses and phoned the restaurant. They found them outside. Nicole lived close by, so she called Mezzaluna and arranged for a waiter, Ron Goldman, to drop them off. Ron, a former model and aspiring actor, was over six feet in height, strong, and practiced in martial arts. He knew Nicole from their gym. They were friends. He was happy to do it. He told a friend to wait at a club for him; he'd be right along. Goldman went home to change, then drove to South Bundy Drive.

Around midnight, a neighbor found Nicole's dog, Kato, wandering in the neighborhood. He took the dog back and discovered a bloodbath.

The only merciful thing that night was that the Simpson children slept through the attack. They never saw the carnage. Both Nicole and Ron had their throats cut; Nicole's wounds were so deep that she was nearly decapitated. Her hands were covered with defensive wounds. Police believe she fought and was punched unconscious so the killer could take care of Ron. Trapped in the corner of the small gated entry, Goldman fought for all he was worth, the killer blocking his only exit. He was stabbed over and over—his hands,

> *"Dad, I said it was a matter of honor,*
> *remember? They called me chicken . . .*
> *you know, chicken?"*
>
> REBEL WITHOUT A CAUSE, 1955

chest, calf, face, and two to the neck. Then the killer turned back to the still-unconscious Nicole. It was butchery.

O.J.—a man who'd been married and divorced twice—hopped a plane to Chicago that night. He got a phone call there. "Your ex-wife is dead." He never asked which one. His hand was cut. He said he'd broken a glass in his hotel room.

The ten-month televised trial became the national pastime. More than 90 percent of TVs in America were tuned in throughout. Race played a huge part. As the verdict was announced, 142 million people listened on radio or watched television. In the end, O.J. walked. And the line between blacks and whites was drawn a little deeper in the sand.

The families of Goldman and Nicole Simpson refused to give up after the acquittal. They brought a civil action of wrongful death against Simpson, and this trial, which began a year later, turned out more successfully for them. In February 1997, a jury found Simpson liable in the deaths of Nicole Simpson and Ronald Goldman and ordered him to pay $25 million in punitive damages to the families. The money has never been paid: Simpson's lawyers argued their client was broke. Simpson now lives on the income from a $4 million pension fund established when he was a professional football player, which cannot be touched by the court. He has custody of his two children.

In the end, Nicole had no way to defend herself. Not divorce. Not 911. Not even a safe-deposit box where she stashed pictures of how she looked after O.J. beat her. What more could Nicole do? She told her sister that O.J. Simpson would kill her and get away with it because he's O.J. Simpson. Yeah, what more's a girl gotta do?

Matchbooks from Mezzaluna disappeared at such a rate that they stopped making them. Also palmed: menus and silverware. Eventually the locals tired of the gawkers and stopped going. It closed in mid-1997.

Nicole's Last Supper

Rigatoni with pepperonata, black olives, spinach, and goat cheese..........$10.00

Robert Blake

Bobby Blake played Mickey, an adorable member of the *Our Gang* series, in the late '30s and early '40s, a darling little guy in overalls with big dark eyes. Life at home was hell. But Hollywood liked him and kept him working in movies like *Humoresque* and *Treasure of the Sierra Madre* into the early '50s. After military service, he returned to Hollywood and managed to do at least a film a year. One, *This Property Is Condemned,* starred Natalie Wood. Mary Badham played Natalie's little sister. Best known for her role as Scout in *To Kill a Mockingbird,* Mary, only about thirteen at the time, recalls Blake helping her through a difficult shoot. "It's amazing how just a tap on the shoulder or a quick hug or a 'good job, kid,' that's it. I remember (him) giving me that confidence when (he) knew I was having a bad time." Sure, Blake had been there. Who better to encourage a child actor than a former one? He knew.

Perseverance paid off. Blake scored big in the '60s with *In Cold Blood, Tell Them*

As Mickey in *Our Gang.* Blake's real name is Michael "Mickey" Gubitosi.

Willie Boy Is Here, Electra Glide in Blue. Then he landed the *Baretta* TV series and the guy was made. Emmys, syndication deals, and all. Sure, he was supposed to be temperamental, unpredictable, a hothead. Johnny Carson often invited Blake on the *Tonight Show.* He loved him because you never knew what was going to happen when he came on. It was great entertainment, but when the series ended, the industry didn't miss Robert Blake. That was OK. He had had a great run. He made some good investments and a comfortable life for himself. He lived quietly. His kids were grown; he had no romantic attachments and was happy picking up the occasional one-night stand at a local bar. That's how he met Bonny Lee Bakley in a jazz club. They began having casual sex.

Bakley, forty-four, had a reputation for sleeping with men in the entertainment business. Friends and relatives described her as "celebrity-obsessed."

"I wanted to be (famous) myself," Bakely said, "and it was too hard. I kept falling for somebody. So I thought, why not fall for a movie star instead of being one? It's more fun. I like being around celebrities. It makes you feel better than other people."

It wasn't the sex she was after as much as it was their bank accounts. For years, she swindled men out of their money through a "lonely-hearts" mail-order nude photo scheme. She participated in *Hustler* magazine's "Great Beaver Hunt." She was married at least nine times, in trouble for drugs and fake identifications. The girl was a grifter. It was too much a part of her to stop.

Bakley became determined to catch herself a celebrity. When she turned up pregnant, she figured she'd nailed one; she just had to figure out which one. She narrowed it down to Christian Brando, son of actor Marlon Brando, or Robert Blake. She hoped for Brando, but told a friend Blake was OK: he wouldn't be around as long.

The baby girl, Rose Lenore Sophia, was born June 2, 2000. After the paternity test proved Blake was the father, he married Bakley on November 11, but it was not your average union. They did not share a bed, not even the main house. Bakley moved into the guesthouse, and she continued her lonely-hearts mail-order career.

Christian Brando warned her, "You better get a handle on that and really think what you're doing, running around sending letters to guys, embezzling money from all these idiots. You're lucky somebody ain't out there to put a bullet in your head."

Brando wasn't crazy. Bonny had stolen the life savings from some of those nine husbands, sad lonely men she took advantage of. She was playing with fire. Blake said he'd seen a prowler hanging around their house and the housekeeper, Lydia, confirmed it, a "mysterious blond, crew-cutted man . . . I know he was afraid . . . he (Blake) said, 'Keep the gate closed, don't leave it open.'"

Judgement Day: The John List Story (1993).

Bonny's relatives say she was scared too, not of a prowler, but of Blake. She expressed fear for her life.

Blake would have paid her off for full custody, but Bakley was clinging to her celebrity marriage. If Blake divorced her, she would leave with the kid. So, no divorce. She may have thought that would protect her; instead, it might have been her death warrant.

On the evening of May 4, 2001, Blake took Bakley out to dinner at Vitello's, an Italian restaurant in Studio City, a suburb in the San Fernando Valley area of Los Angeles. Blake lived nearby and had taken his family there for years. "We always parked two blocks away (from the restaurant)," said his daughter, "because after a meal at Vitello's we always wanted to walk."

That's why Blake parked two blocks away when he dined with Bonny. They returned to the car and he realized he'd left his gun inside, the one he carried for protection. He left her on this deserted street while he walked back to the restaurant. Witnesses in the restaurant say Blake didn't retrieve anything. He drank a glass of water and left. When he returned to the car, Bonny had been fatally shot in the head and upper body as she sat in their car.

According to court papers, an informant tipped police within two weeks of the slaying that Blake had offered $100,000 for someone to "bump her off." The documents, which include search warrants and affidavits, quote witnesses as saying Blake solicited two stuntmen to kill Bakley. One stuntman told of being taken on a tour of Blake's home while the actor pointed out areas where his wife

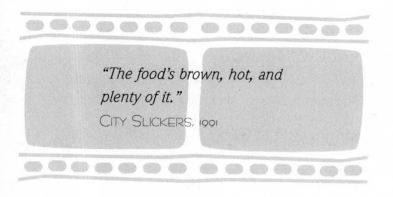

could be killed. The other stuntman told of being driven past Vitello's where Blake suggested she could be shot while seated in a car. Police waited nearly a year to arrest Blake while they searched for physical evidence to support the stuntmen's accounts. They found little until March, when they located a prepaid telephone card used to call the men.

Blake's bodyguard and assistant, Earle Caldwell, had accompanied the couple on recent trips to Las Vegas and Sequoia National Park. The police searched Caldwell's jeep and found an ominous shopping list: Drano, duct tape, old rugs, and shovels. The prosecutors considered it excellent evidence of intent.

The LAPD concluded that Robert Blake and Earle Caldwell were responsible for the death of Bonny Lee Bakley. After almost a year of investigation, Robert Blake was arrested in April 2002 and charged with murder with "special circumstances": solicitation of murder, conspiracy, and the special circumstance of lying in wait. His bodyguard, Earle Caldwell, was charged with conspiracy to murder. Blake was denied bail, but he put up $1 million to have Caldwell released. The prosecution announced that it would not seek the death penalty.

Blake was held until March 2003. "I never thought I'd make eleven months in a cement box," said the sixty-nine-year-old on the day of his release. "This is God's day. He's never let me down." His black hair had turned white and he'd dropped a lot of weight. Blake looked like he'd been through hell. The judge said Blake would have to stay at one residence, have electronic monitoring, and surrender his passport.

"I believe the real killer is still out there," said Harland Braun, Blake's attorney. "My prediction is this will never be solved."

Meanwhile, former NFL star and accused wife murderer O.J. Simpson says various television outlets have contacted him to help cover Blake's pending trial. Simpson said he would "love to do it." For obvious reasons, Simpson said he has "a lot of insight" into murder trials.

After Bonny Lee Bakley's murder, business at Vitello's increased 30 percent and menus starting disappearing, especially when there was a certain daily special.

Fusilli e Minestra alla Robert Blake

Corkscrew pasta, garlic, spinach, and fresh tomatoes in olive oil.

Side Dishes

Lupe Velez 201
David Niven 207
Bobby Darin 211

Lupe Velez

If you repeat something often enough, it becomes the truth, at least in Hollywood. That's how Lupe Velez came to be stuck with one of the most mortifying legends of Tinseltown, so fantastic it simply cannot be true. At first glance, her story seems an all too familiar Hollywood fairy tale gone bad: beautiful star, not so young at thirty-four, pregnant by a heel who refused to marry her, career on the skids. Here's where the legend comes in: She decided to end it all Hollywood-style, filling her house with flowers, ordering a lavish last supper, a Mexican feast, none of which she could pay for. She called her two best pals to cry and hug and chow down. Afterward, she bid them a final farewell, wrote a note to the heel, took a bottle of pills, and laid herself on satin sheets amid the flowers, to be found in peaceful repose. After a time, Lupe woke up sick to her stomach. The Mexican food and the pills didn't mix. She stumbled into the bathroom, slipped, and fell headfirst into her toilet bowl where, unconscious, she drowned. Now I ask ya, what are the odds?

Now, if you've been paying attention up until now, you know that when a celebrity is found dead, the police are the last ones called. No way in hell would Lupe's loved ones let her be found that way. They would have cleaned her up and laid her out. Gossip columnist and friend to Velez, Louella Parsons, reported the death scene to millions of fans this way: "Lupe never looked lovelier as she lay there as if slumbering, looking like a happy child taking a nappy." That's a movie star death if ever there was one. The real story lies somewhere between the two.

The exotic Lupe Velez specialized in playing flashy, temperamental ladies on screen while her volatile, offscreen romances heated up the headlines of the '30s. She was a little package of dynamite: 5 feet tall, 109 pounds soaking wet, and 37-26-35—*ay yi yi!* She made seventy pictures in seventeen years and made love to some of the most fascinating men in Hollywood: John Gilbert, Clayton Moore, Steve Crane, Eric Maria Remarquez. Striking, successful, a gifted comedienne, and quite the party girl, Lupe was popular and professional. You'd be hard-pressed to find anybody with a bad word to say about her. She named her hacienda in Beverly Hills *Casa Felicitas*—"Happy House." And she was happy there, for a time.

On the rebound from a stormy affair with Gary Cooper, Lupe married Johnny Weissmuller in 1933. Tarzan and his mate fought like jungle cats, and Johnny kept the makeup men working overtime, covering scratches and love bites. Their public fights were legendary. One night at Ciro's, Lupe was wowing them on the dance floor. She spun so fiercely, her dress flew up and—oops, forgot my panties!—Johnny went ape and dumped their dinner in her lap. The guy needed to get a sense of humor . . . like he wasn't lifting his loincloth to any girl that would take a peek. They divorced in 1938.

In the 1940s, Lupe starred with Leon Errol in a series of "Mexican Spitfire" comedies written just for her, a parody of her own persona. She bounced from one "B" list romance to another. In 1944, she was seeing Harald Ramond, twenty-seven, a hanger-on looking for a way into the business, nothing more.

In July of '44, she was pregnant. First, Lupe decided to have the baby and called Lolly Parsons to announce their engagement. Harald said he could only marry her in a fake ceremony. Said his ex-wife would sue him for plenty if he married a rich movie star. Or maybe she wasn't his ex yet. Maybe hot-blooded Lupe was furious to find out there was another woman. The hell with Harald and his fake marriage! She planned to go to Santa Barbara or to Mexico to have the baby and have one of her married sisters, Josefina, pose as the mother. Then Lupe would adopt the baby and bring it to Los Angeles. Josie said she and Lupe discussed this plan in front of Harald.

By December, she was six or seven months pregnant. After the birth—in about two months—she was to tour in a musical revue at close to $1,000 a week for a year. She also left movie contracts pending. Her estate was worth $750,000. She was not in financial trouble.

> *"When I was a little girl, I used to go home for lunch every day, and I'd pretend that my mother was a waitress in a roadside café. I'll have a side order, ma'am. A side order consists of a white-meat tuna, a dollop of mayonnaise, some carrot strips, and potato chips. And then I'd sit at the counter . . . and ignore her."*
>
> WITHOUT YOU I'M NOTHING, 1990

December 12 was the day of Lupe's saint, the Virgin of Guadalupe, the most beloved and revered of all saints in Mexico. It's a holy day of great celebration and fiesta. Lupe, convent-schooled and deeply religious, celebrated in the traditional way, by filling the house with flowers and feasting on a traditional Mexican meal. The flowers and food—all paid for—were for the holiday, not a planned grand finale.

The evening of the fourteenth, she attended the premiere of her latest film, *Nana.* She invited her two closest friends, Estelle Taylor (the ex–Mrs. Jack Dempsey) and Benita (Mrs. Jack) Oakie. Taylor later told the press, "Lupe told me about the baby. She said she had plenty of opportunity to get rid of it. But she said, 'It's my baby, I couldn't commit murder and still live myself. I would rather kill myself.'" Lupe told Estelle that since she was a little girl, she'd had to fight for everything she got. She was tired of fighting now, tired of fighting the world. No question, the girl was low. Maybe the ladies had a midnight snack, but there was more brandy consumed than food. Her friends stayed until

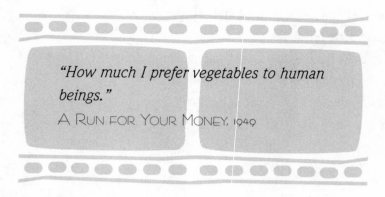

"How much I prefer vegetables to human beings."
A RUN FOR YOUR MONEY, 1949

3:00 A.M. Lupe begged Benita to stay overnight, a sure sign that she still did not plan to do herself in.

But something changed. Sometime after three o'clock, things got the better of her. Intoxicated, exhausted, and alone, she gave up the struggle.

Lupe wrote two notes, one to Harald asking how he could have "faked his love" for her and the baby. She also left a note to her secretary, Beulah Kinder. Lupe called Beulah Mommy and clearly cared for her; she left her one-third of her $750,000 estate. She knew it would be "Mommy" who would find her body. She drank brandy and swallowed all the pills she had left in a bottle of Seconal. Lupe had taken Seconal for ten years, and you can bet she'd taken it with Mexican food before.

Beulah found her around seven that morning. Her account is nothing if not believable. Lupe's body lay sprawled on the bedroom floor, near the bathroom. Her hands were underneath her as if she had tried to get up. In front of her was a glass she'd been carrying, the liquid spilled out. In her right hand was a picture of her late father, which she had taken from her bureau. The phone on her nightstand was off the hook. Next to it were the notes, dated the fourteenth. An empty bottle of Seconal held them in place. If you believe what you read in the papers, doctors and police worked on Miss Velez with an inhalator for an hour before a police surgeon pronounced her dead. Lupe had ingested pills no more than four hours earlier. It was possible her vital signs were imperceptible, so they worked on her. If she drowned or suffocated, there would have been no reviving her.

Ramond seemed remorseful, even anguished. He said that it was a terrible mix-up.

Lupe and Johnny, Palm Springs '32.
They fought like wildcats in public and
between the sheets.

A quiet moment for the high-spirited star.

He'd never said he faked his love, only
that he'd have to fake the marriage. That
little agreement he'd had her sign to that
effect weeks earlier should have made
that clear enough, the louse. Seems he left no illusions.

Screen siren and former Cooper girlfriend Clara Bow told writer Robert Slatzer that
Gary was in complete shock, screaming and crying that he would kill that S.O.B.,
Ramond. "Personally, I never believed Lupe's child was fathered by the foreign boyfriend
because he didn't mean that much to Lupe," she continued. "I think she blamed him to
protect Gary." When she asked Coop if the kid could be his, he admitted it was possible.
Could it have hurt him? Sure. But it destroyed Ramond. Hollywood had his number and
nobody called it. He disappeared without a trace.

Lupe was not broke and her career, though not what it had been, was still very much
alive. She never planned her death. There was no funereal floral display, no farewell feast
of spicy food, which, in all likelihood, means no upset stomach, no fatal run to the bathroom. No death by toilet. Once and for all, let's close the lid on that one.

Here are a few staples at any Mexican feast.

Spanish Rice

12 servings

1½ ounces oil
1   yellow onion, diced
2   garlic cloves, finely chopped
2   quarts water
2   green bell peppers, seeded
    and diced
2   16-ounce cans whole peeled
    tomatoes or crushed
    tomatoes, drained
1½ tablespoons chicken stock
1   teaspoon salt
4   cups long-grain white rice

In a large saucepan heat the oil. Add the onion and garlic and sauté for 1 minute. Add the water, bell peppers, tomatoes, and chicken stock, and boil for 10 minutes. Add the salt. Lower the heat and continue boiling for 5 minutes until the peppers and onion are soft. Add the rice and stir for 2 minutes. Cover the pot, lower the heat, and keep covered until the broth is absorbed, about 15 minutes.

Refried Beans

6 servings

2   cups dry pinto beans
10 cups of water
2   tablespoons salt
4   ounces vegetable oil
2   ounces Cheddar cheese,
    grated
2   ounces Monterey Jack
    cheese, grated

In a gallon pot, combine the beans, water, and salt. Cook on high heat for 90 minutes, until the beans are tender. Reduce the water to a negligible amount. Add the heated vegetable oil and both cheeses. Mash with a potato masher until thick and rich.

David Niven

Everybody liked David Niven. He was everything the Yanks loved about the Brits: dapper, charming, funny—and get a load of that fancy accent. He and best pal Errol Flynn got around town pretty good. Niven made quick progress with his career, too. It was a good thing he had a lot of friends and fans; he needed them like nothing else in 1945.

Niven was going places in movies after just four years in Tinseltown. So he surprised everybody when he walked out on his contract at Goldwyn to enlist. It was only 1939—he was the first major star to join up and Hollywood missed him like mischief. He was briefly involved with British Intelligence, then he transferred to the Commandoes and landed on the beaches at Normandy in 1944. Colonel Niven was awarded the American Legion of Merit, the highest American order a noncitizen can earn—presented by General Dwight D. Eisenhower himself.

Overseas, David met a honey of a WAAF named Primula Rollo. She was no match

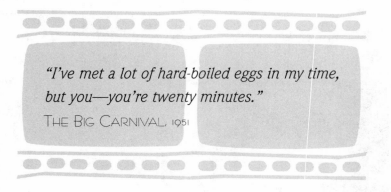

for the Niven charm. It only took ten days for him to get her to accept his proposal. The guy had a gift. "She was an absolute darling," said Michael Trubshaw, Niven's best man and lifelong friend, "the perfect English rose. David used to always say he was the luckiest man in the world, but it was only when he met Primmie that I began to believe him."

The happy couple had two beautiful boys, and friends who knew him best said this was far and away his happiest time. Niven had been away from Hollywood for almost six years. With the end of the war, he brought his family to Los Angeles to return to his career.

Just two months after the Nivens arrived, Annabella and Tyrone Power gave a little soirée for Primmie. She loved Ty—name me a woman who didn't. It was a casual group, most of David's best pals: Lilli Palmer and Rex Harrison, Gene Tierney and Oleg Cassini, Richard Greene and Patricia Medina, Cesar Romero. Primmie had never been to a clambake in digs like this—a beautiful, rambling Spanish manor in the hoity-toity community of Bel Air. Al Jolson built the place in the late '20s as a summer home for bride number three, Ruby Keeler. When they divorced in '39, Power scooped it up, and he and Annabella held their nuptials in the courtyard. Mrs. Niven was on cloud nine.

The group enjoyed a few cocktails around the pool and Power manned the barbeque. After the sun went down, Annabella suggested they move inside.

Tomorrow was a workday, but before the party broke up, somebody suggested a game of "sardines"—hide-and-seek English-style—played in the dark. The English thought anything done in the dark was naughty. Primmie was "it." She closed her eyes and everybody ran. David groped his way upstairs and hid under a bed. Ty hid behind an overstuffed chair in the living room. He heard a door open and shut. Primmie moved farther away from him and he stifled a laugh. He heard another door open and shut. Then he heard a startled cry and several muffled thuds. He jumped up, ran to the cellar door, and switched on the light. Primmie was lying at the bottom of the steps. She took the cellar door for a coat closet and fell backward down twenty steps. She died the next day, at age twenty-eight. "Something went out of David when Primmie died, and it never returned," recalled friend Doug Fairbanks Jr. "It was just an awful time."

Forty-five years later, I found myself having dinner in the house, but I didn't know it was *the* house. The owner told me about her home's rich history. When she mentioned the Power-Annabella wedding, I leaped to my feet. "This is the house where Primmie Niven was killed!" My hostess regarded me with scorn, but what did I care? I had to see the stairs. Reluctantly, she led the way.

It was easy to see how Mrs. Niven had mistaken the basement door for a coat closet; I would have, too. And in the dark, Primmie never stood a chance. I thought about that night, her first Hollywood party, giggling in the dark looking for Tyrone Power. It must have all been so exciting. I stared down the steep stairs to the cold, cement floor and a chill ran through me. "You're morbid," my hostess said with all the disgust she could manage. She turned away.

Her boyfriend motioned me over, out of earshot. "You know," he whispered, "even after all these years, our dog won't go near these stairs. When we open the door, he runs in the other direction."

"I'm no good at being noble, but it doesn't take much to see that the problems of three little people don't amount to a hill of beans in this crazy world. Someday you'll understand that. Now, now . . . Here's looking at you kid."

CASABLANCA, 1942

David Niven went through a dark time. Pal Clark Gable had lost his wife, Carole Lombard, in a plane crash. He was the only one who could comfort him. Eventually, Niven climbed out of that hole to live a full and happy life. When his appetite returned, he cooked up this hearty meal.

Red Rice Mold

4	tablespoons chopped pimientos
1	tablespoon grated onion
1	teaspoon Worcestershire sauce
3	cups boiled rice
½	cup olive oil
¾	cup milk
2	eggs, well beaten
	Pimiento strips and hard-boiled egg for garnish

Preheat the oven to 350°. Combine the pimientos, onion, and Worcestershire sauce with the boiled rice. Add the olive oil, then the milk and eggs. Turn into a well-greased ring mold, place the mold in a pan of hot water, and bake for 1 hour and 15 minutes. Unmold onto a large circular platter. Around the base of the ring, place small bundles of asparagus tips at equal intervals, laying a strip of pimiento across each bundle. Between the bundles of asparagus, place slices of hard-boiled egg. Fill the center of the ring with creamed shrimp or crab meat.

Bobby Darin

Bobby Darin and finger-snappin' go together like martinis and olives. He put the swing in swinger, baby. He traveled strictly in the fast lane and took it straight to the top. But a dark turn sent him skidding out of control to a dead end . . . real dead.

Darin's career is a '50s fairy tale come true: Poor kid from an Italian neighborhood in the Bronx makes it big, really big. By seventeen, he was already singing in clubs. Mom and sis were so proud. His first big hit—which he wrote in fifteen minutes on a dare—came at twenty-two. "Splish, Splash" soared to number three on the charts in '58. At twenty-three, he announced his plans to be a legend by twenty-five. At twenty-five, his version of "Mack the Knife" stayed on the hit list for six months, nine weeks at number one. He won Best New Artist and Record of the Year Grammys for 1959, beating out the original king of cool, Sinatra. When the press asked him how it felt to beat the Boss, Bobby replied matter-of-factly, "I hope to surprise Sinatra in everything he's ever done."

Who the hell did this guy think he was? You gotta be nuts to say you're going after Sinatra. Bobby Darin came off like an egomaniac. Nobody knew the cat might not make it to twenty-six. Darin was in a hurry to make his mark because of a death sentence he got when he was just eight years old. Rheumatic fever and subsequent heart damage reduced his life expectancy. Mid-twenties was about as much as he could hope for. At least his mom saw his success. She died in '59, leaving Bobby and sister Nina.

The swinging '60s brought Bobby to the left coast to conquer Hollywood. He wanted to do everything: singing, acting, business. While shooting *Come September* with eighteen-year-old Sandra Dee, a romance blossomed between the two teen idols. They were the darlings of the fan magazines as the press photographed their every move. The "dream lovers" married in December. The following year, they had a son.

The Darins found married life a challenge. One superstar ego is difficult; two is impossible. Sandra was a young, pampered star. She didn't enjoy tagging along after Bobby from club to club like some sort of "hanger-on." He loved performing live, but she pushed him to give up nightclubbing. In '63, he did, hoping it would save his troubled marriage; it didn't. Three years later, he made a sensational comeback. A racehorse has to race, baby. Divorce soon followed.

Life got a lot more serious. Bobby tuned in, turned on, and became deeply committed to Robert F. Kennedy's presidential campaign. When Kennedy was assassinated in

Bobby and Sandra Dee got *That Funny Feeling* in 1956, but it wouldn't last.

"Well, that's cuz he only had one. I checked.
Plenty of meat, only one potato."

PSYCHO BEACH PARTY, 2000

'68, a devastated Darin felt he had to do something, had to say something. He entertained political ambitions and was courted by the Democrats. That's when his sister,
Nina, dropped a bombshell. If someone were to dig into his past, they'd find a deep, dark
family secret: "I'm not your sister. I'm your mother." In 1936, Nina entered the hospital
as his mother, but left as his sister. Bobby's grandmother took on the role of mother. They
moved to a new neighborhood and never told anyone, not even Bobby. Darin couldn't
believe what he was hearing. He completely flipped out. His entire life was built on a lie.
Nina had denied her own son all those years. Part of him hated her for that. He never
felt comfortable with her again and never acknowledged her as his mother.

Bobby was on a real bad trip. Losing Kennedy and then his family knocked him for
a loop. He questioned everything, reassessed his priorities. Material things lost all value.
He sold his house and most of his possessions, choosing to live out of his car. He called
himself Bob, grew sideburns, and sang protest songs in Vegas. Afterward, he would drive
into the desert, pull out a sleeping bag, and cook up something simple over a campfire.
Friends and fans didn't know what to make of the change. He bombed big-time.

Finally, the '70s brought him some peace. He found happiness in a new marriage. He
donned the tux and toupée, returned to Vegas, and gave the people what they wanted.
They welcomed him back with enthusiasm. The brashness was gone. In its place were
experience and maturity . . . and that finger-snappin' jazz. From cocky kid to established
artist, Darin emerged as a compassionate survivor. But now, just as it all came together,
his health fell apart. In '71, Bobby needed open-heart surgery. He returned to the scene

seven months later in a hot summer variety show, then a weekly series. He belted out a tune, then retreated offstage for oxygen. Audiences never knew how sick he was.

In December of '73, Bobby needed another heart operation; this time, he didn't make it. He was dead at thirty-seven. Fans were shocked and saddened, even Sinatra. But there were no sentimental goodbyes. Bobby wanted no funeral at all, not even a grave. He donated his body to UCLA Medical School. In 1990, Darin was posthumously inducted into the Rock and Roll Hall of Fame. And the legend lives on. Go, man, go.

Singers and Swingers in the Kitchen *declared that Bobby's "absolutely most favorite meal is a rare steak, baked potato, and his 'special spinach.'"*

Special Spinach

6 servings

2	packages frozen chopped spinach (hey, it was the '60s . . .)
3	tablespoons butter or margarine
2	tablespoons finely chopped onion
2	tablespoons flour
1	cup milk or light cream
½	teaspoon salt
⅛	teaspoon ground nutmeg

Follow the instructions on the spinach boxes; drain thoroughly when cooked. Melt the butter over low, low heat; add the onion and cook till it's soft, stirring every so often. Remove from the heat; mix in the flour—no lumps now! Add the milk slowly and cook until it's thick. Stir in the salt and nutmeg and then mix this sauce into the drained spinach. Heat a bit longer over a low flame.

Candy Desserts

Carole Landis 217

George Reeves 225

Jean Seberg 229

Diane Linkletter 233

Divine 239

Carole Landis

One of Tinseltown's best-known tales of unrequited amour is the sad story of pretty Carole Landis. Career on the skids, divorce from husband number four in the wings, deep in debt, and a lover who gives her the Fuller—the brush, baby, the brush. Nobody ever doubted that Carole Landis offed herself. No one even blinked. That made the studio's cover job a lot easier. So why was there a cover-up? What was there to hide?

Armed with beauty, ambition, and 37-24-35, Carole quit school at fifteen and moved to San Francisco to get some "experience." She danced the hula at the Royal Hawaiian Café, though gossipmongers say it was mostly the horizontal kind. A year later, she married a young actor, Irving Wheeler, who introduced his bride to Busby Berkeley. The famed director immediately cast shapely blonde Carole in a bit part in his current picture. She ended up with a dance solo and a marriage that lasted twenty-five days . . . hmmm. Carole's star began to rise with *One Million B.C., Topper Returns,* and her autobiographical adventures of entertaining the troops, *Four Jills and a Jeep.* During the year she spent overseas, Carole contracted malaria and suffered from a recurring infection the rest of her short life.

There were two more marriages, one lasting two months, the third for two years. For a tomato labeled as gold-digging, man-chasing, and promiscuous, she sure never married money. A contract at Twentieth Century-Fox brought some good roles, but more rumors plagued Carole, primarily the servicing-the-boss kind. The studio didn't renew because of them, and no big studio would touch her after that. Her fourth dog of a husband, Horace Schmidlapp (the name alone should have served as a warning), spent most of his time and money on the East Coast. Carole got nothing from him. (After her death, the heel sued for half her $35,000 estate; he went away for $15,000 cash.) Things looked bleak for the twenty-nine-year-old. For luck in love, she wore all her wedding rings stacked on one finger. She consoled herself in the arms of "good friend" Rex Harrison, who was married to actress Lilli Palmer. Carole's maid, Fannie Bolden, said Miss Landis had pictures of Harrison all over her bedroom. She also said she thought that Miss Landis expected Harrison to leave his wife for her.

According to the "official" version: On July 4, 1948, Carole had a few friends over for a swim party at her $100,000 home, up for sale in the divorce. It was Sunday, and Fannie had the day off. After the guests left, Carole showered, dressed, and prepared dinner for Sexy Rexy, as she had often done during the run of their affair and nearly every night that week. (Bolden later told the press Harrison "ate like a pig.") But apparently this night, Carole pressed for a commitment. Rexy said it wasn't going to happen and left at 9:00 P.M. for the home of a friend, Roland Culver. But that night, poor Carole wasn't having any more rejection. No, that Fourth of July, she declared her independence for good.

She cried; she drank. She lay down for a while. When she got up, she knew what she had to do. She took down all of Rex's pictures and gathered his letters and mementos, putting them in two small cases. She drove to Roland Culver's and left them at a side gate. Harrison—who never admitted to the affair—speculated years later in his autobiography that sweet, considerate Carole, in her darkest moment, had thought of him (who else?), thought to spare him a scandal by removing all connection to him from her home.

The next morning, Fannie knocked on the bedroom door every hour after she arrived, and Rex called half a dozen times. Neither got an answer. Finally Rex drove there and, when Fannie was in the kitchen, he slipped into Carole's bedroom. Carole lay on the bathroom floor in front of the sink. The cabinet underneath was open. Her head rested on a jewel box, her hands propped underneath her as if she'd tried to get up. Later, friends interpreted this to mean that Carole had changed her mind, that she was trying to call for help. Anyway, Rexy called Fannie and made a big display of finding Carole.

"Oh, darling, why'd you do it?" he wailed. Too bad Fannie wasn't a member of the Academy. She thought it was quite a performance. She watched as Rex went straight to a note on the vanity.

> *Dearest Mommie: I'm sorry, really sorry, to put you through this. But there is no way to avoid it. I love you, darling. You have been the most wonderful mom ever. And that applies to all our family. I love each and every one of them dearly. Everything goes to you. Look in the files and there is a will which decrees everything. Goodbye, my angel. Pray for me. Your baby*

Although Harrison swore he called the police, he never did; no call was logged until Fannie got a neighbor to call. Rex did call Lilli, who flew immediately from New York to stand by her louse—er, husband.

Police investigating the death scene concluded Landis had lain down on her bed at some point that night. After 3:00 A.M., they conjecture, still dressed in her dinner clothes, she penciled the note to her mother on her monogrammed stationery and propped it on her vanity. In the bathroom, she sat on the floor, opened the cupboard under the sink, and pulled out a small envelope. She poured out a handful of Seconals and swallowed them. As the pills took effect, she rested her head on a little jewel box. She died there.

Landis had considered suicide in the past and, certainly, all the ingredients were there this time; it seemed pretty open and shut. But there was some flimflam around her death that makes you wonder who was hiding what.

Aquatic actress Esther Williams confirms it. "His affair with Carole Landis was the worst-kept secret in Hollywood," she writes in her autobiography. What's more, she says

Rex and Lilli remained civilized before the cameras throughout the scandal.
(*The Four Poster*, 1952)

she was at a barbeque at Rex's in Los Angeles that Sunday and both Rex and Lilli were there. Rex left later for a "rehearsal." He never came back, at least not before 2:00 A.M., when Esther went home.

According to Williams, the studio orchestrated "a platoon of people (who) could account for every minute of Rex's time." Lilli stuck to the story—even years later in her own autobiography—that she flew in the morning of July 6 from New York. "No one who attended that Fourth of July party denied that Lilli was in New York. Including me. I knew 'the rules,'" Williams said.

Some believe Carole left a note for Harrison, too. Alexander Walker writes, "A former Los Angeles policeman, an officer long retired from the force, says he recalls seeing the note and it was a three-line lover's farewell to Rex Harrison."

Lilli Palmer backs this up in her autobiography, saying lawyers told them a policeman had removed a note from Carole's clenched hand and kept it. It was supposed to contain something highly compromising. He wanted $500 for it.

"Five hundred dollars was a lot of money in those days, especially for us, whose con-tracts were about to be canceled. On the other hand, what could the note contain? An indictment? A cry of despair? We went back to the lawyers and said we'd chance it. The policeman could do what he liked with the note. . . . A little while later they were back with an envelope. . . . They'd been able to make the man see reason. We opened the envelope and a small piece of crumpled paper fell out. On it, a few almost illegible words: 'The cat has a sore paw. She must go to the vet.'" Carole's mother told the press the cat was perfectly fine.

Rumors of a third note were started by Harry Lang, in the *L.A. Examiner:*

"And late yesterday, that maid, Fannie Mae Bolden, revealed that after the police had arrived, a woman friend of Miss Landis, who had in the meantime talked with Harrison, came into the kitchen and said: 'Fannie Mae, you must remember that Miss Carole said in the note she left that you must not talk about this to anybody.'

"The maid added: 'I know that there was nothing like that in the one note that Miss Landis left for her mother.'"

And though Carole was quite specific about her will in that note, no will was ever found. By the time police arrived, her files had been rifled through. Several papers known to be in her possession were missing, including the will.

Then there's the Seconal. Carole had no prescription for it, and her doctor denied giv-ing her any without a prescription. Landis hadn't been prescribed sleeping pills for some-thing like two years. No Seconal pill bottle was found in the house, only an envelope that had contained pills, found in her hand. The envelope still had one pill in it—a Nembutal. In '49, Seconal had no odor, no taste, and no "expecto-rant" qualities. You might take it with a drink, but you also wouldn't know if you'd taken it *in* a drink—and there

> *"I was always in the kitchen. I felt as though I'd been born in a kitchen and lived there all my life except for the few hours it took to get married.*
> MILDRED PIERCE, 1945

Ambitious gold digger or maligned victim?

was no way for the medical examiner to know either. (Nowadays, Seconal has a bitter taste and is laced with ipecac to induce vomiting and prevent overdose. In fact, it was partly as a result of Landis's death that these properties were added to sleeping pills).

So, an "unofficial" scenario of that fateful night might go this way: Rex broke up with Carole; she became hysterical; he gave her something to calm down or sleep—on her bed. While she slept, he took all his photos and love notes and left them at Roland Culver's back gate; if Lilli really was home, he couldn't take them there. Then he returns to check on Carole. While he was away, she woke up, all alone. All his pictures were gone as if he'd never existed. Deeply distraught, in a drugged state, she took more pills—a fatal dose. Harrison returned to find her dead on the bathroom floor. Now he has to remove anything that pointed to him. If you believe Esther Williams, the studio sent help to go through the files before the police or Fannie ever got there.

One thing seems clear: Harrison was the last person to see Carole alive and the first person to see her dead. None of this proves that Harrison had anything to do with her death, but you gotta admit there's more here than meets the eye. Hollywood thought so too; they ostracized Harrison for the two-timing worm he was. Much of that was out of guilt for their part in her death; Hollywood had turned its back on Carole Landis years before.

Carole was once quoted as saying, "I have no intention of ending my career in a rooming house, with full scrapbooks and an empty stomach." Well, her stomach was full. Carole's last supper with Harrison was tossed salad, cold roast chicken, and chilled lemon chiffon pie. Harrison drank Scotch; Landis, white wine. The Joe Mooney Quartet, a popular jazz group, was on the phonograph. Ironically, the song was "A Warm Kiss and a Cold Heart."

Lemon Chiffon Pie

1	9-inch pie crust
2¼	teaspoons unflavored gelatin
½	cup strained fresh lemon juice
1	teaspoon grated lemon zest
⅓	cup plus 1 tablespoon sugar
4	large eggs, separated
¼	teaspoon cream of tartar
½	cup sugar

Prepare the pie crust. Pour ¼ cup water into a small, heavy saucepan. Sprinkle the gelatin over the top and let stand for 5 minutes. Whisk in ½ cup water, the lemon juice, lemon zest, sugar, and egg yolks. Stirring constantly with a wooden spoon or rubber spatula, heat over medium heat until it begins to steam and coats the spoon heavily. Do not simmer! Immediately pour the mixture into a large bowl and refrigerate for 45 minutes to 1 hour or until small mounds form when dropped from a spoon. Do not let it set.

Beat the egg whiles until foamy. Add the cream of tartar and continue to beat until soft peaks form. Gradually beat in the sugar.

Increase speed and beat until the peaks are stiff and glossy. Using a large rubber spatula, gently fold the egg whites into the gelatin mixture. Spoon the filling into the crust, mounding it in the center, and refrigerate for at least 4 hours or up to 24 hours.

George Reeves

Faster than a speeding bullet . . . what a crock. Superman was brought down by a slug from a German Luger. But who was on the other end of that gun? Well . . . that's the question, kiddo; that is the question.

Reeves was a hunk—tall, dark, and handsome; a good pal, great between the sheets and in the kitchen too; this guy really *was* Superman. As "The Man of Steel," he flew into thirty countries from 1953 to 1957. But he was so closely identified with the role, his career slammed shut like a steel trap when the show ended. He convinced producers to give him a break—a big role in the much-anticipated *From Here to Eternity,* but preview audiences hooted and hollered the minute Superman came on-screen. The studio was forced to cut his role to virtually nothing. The rest of Tinseltown followed suit. A year and a half flew by with no offers of work. But that didn't mean George wasn't busy. Oh no, he had his hands full.

His dog was stolen, his car tampered with twice. Somebody was out to get him . . . and they did.

With no work offered, Reeves created some. Under the banner of his newly formed production company, he planned to direct and star in a science fiction film. And *Superman* was to return to the air in 1960 with new scripts and a beefed-up salary. But costar Jack "Jimmy Olsen" Larson believes Reeves had grown to hate the role. "His costume was wool. It was hot and uncomfortable and he hated it." And though George was in great shape, he was getting older. Larson said he needed a girdle to squeeze into those tights and he constantly had to dye his graying hair. Sounds like playing Superman was a real pain in the cape.

Reeves found comfort in the arms of a lot of women, and soon just one woman. Toni Mannix was the sleep-around wife of Loew's VP Eddie Mannix, a man with mob connections and an erectile problem. He looked the other way when Toni fooled around. He looked the other way a lot. But Toni quit other guys when she fell for George. Eddie even signed the checks for a Jaguar sports car, a house in Beverly Hills, and countless other "friendship gifts" Toni gave George. So it's no surprise she did not take it well when George announced his plans to marry ex–New York showgirl Lenore Lemmon, notorious for being eighty-sixed from half the clubs in New York for fighting.

About the time Reeves started making wedding plans, round-the-clock nuisance calls began—mostly hang-ups—up to twenty a day. Reeves filed a complaint against Toni with the Beverly Hills PD, but she told them she was getting the same calls. Twice after that, George discovered suspicious mechanical failures with his car and his beloved Schnauzer dog was stolen. Reeves was worried enough to turn his home into an arsenal of weapons, including two knives, a club, a .22 pistol, and a Luger.

On George's last night, Lemmon later told the cops that they had been toasting the future with a house-guest. Around 12:30 A.M.,

the inebriated trio went to bed. A half-hour later, they were all awakened by two friends even more bombed than they were. Lenore and her friend poured drinks all around, but George went back to bed. Then, a single shot rang out.

According to the official version, Reeves was nude, sprawled faceup on the bed—a suicide. There was a bullet hole above his right ear and an empty cartridge under him. The fatal bullet was lodged in the ceiling. The Luger pistol lay on the floor nearby. Funny thing is, most self-inflicted gunshots force the victim forward and facedown while the shell drops behind. And another thing, Reeves had no powder burns on the side of his head, so the gun had to have been almost a foot and a half away. For George to have offed

Reeves with the *Superman* cast—did a return to the show spell disaster?

himself means he had to hold the gun near or below his waist while tilting his head to the side over it. Who kills himself like that? It's not exactly a sure thing. Now if two people were fighting for the gun and it fired . . . bingo, there's your speeding bullet.

We may never know exactly what happened that night. Was the thought of returning to the role of Superman so depressing that George killed himself? Did a jealous Toni Mannix have him killed? Or was it Lenore? Did he decide to call off the wedding and stick with his golden goose? With her well-publicized temper fueled by alcohol, she could have pulled the trigger as they fought. Someone bought the cops because they stood by the suicide theory, despite all the evidence to the contrary. Case closed; no further investigation. Have a cookie.

In a November 4, 1955, featured column in the Phoenix Gazette *called "My Favorite Recipe," George Reeves had this interesting entry: Corn Flake Cookies. I think it may have had something to do with the fact that one of the sponsors for the show was Kellogg's Corn Flakes.*

Superman Cookies

¼	pound butter, softened
½	cup white sugar
½	cup light brown sugar
1	large egg, beaten
1½	cups flour
¼	teaspoon baking soda
½	cup coarsely grated chocolate
1	cup corn flakes

Preheat the oven to 375°. Cream the butter and sugars together. Blend in the beaten egg. Blend in the flour ½ cup at a time. Add the soda dissolved in 1 tablespoon hot water. Add the grated chocolate and corn flakes. Add nuts if desired.

Drop by teaspoonfuls onto a greased cookie sheet and bake for 10 to 12 minutes. Remove from the sheet and cool on a cake rack.

Jean Seberg

Small-town girl makes good in the talent search of the decade. In 1957, big-shot director Otto Preminger searched the globe for the perfect girl to star in his epic spectacle of the life of Joan of Arc. Eighteen thousand girls answered the call, but wispy Iowa University student Jean Seberg was plucked from obscurity and shot to overnight stardom. The next day Ed Sullivan introduced her to 60 million TV viewers. Even with a mountain of pre-publicity, the picture flopped. Preminger gave Jean one more chance the following year, as a manipulative teenage temptress in *Bonjour Tristesse.* She did alright, but the guy was a monster to her. He humiliated her in screaming rants on the set, and she attempted suicide more than once. Then he dropped her, left her in France.

Seberg, unsophisticated, unworldly, barely twenty, established residence in Paris in 1958. She quickly married handsome filmmaker François Moreuil "for ridiculous reasons," she later said. But there's a reason for everything. Moreuil was part of the scene.

He introduced her around to his crop of struggling avant-garde filmmakers. One, Jean-Luc Godard, asked her to star in his first feature. Made on a shoestring, *Breathless* left the world of cinema just that. Godard became the leader of the New Wave of French filmmakers. And Jean was their darling, an instant presence—shining, frantic, clean-scrubbed, articulate, fragile. The 5'4", 108-pound gamine became an instant cinematic sex kitten, pursued by men, imitated by women, a luminous star of the late '50s and early '60s.

"I suppose the mystique about me, the aura of serenity, is due to my upbringing, to some kind of puritanical self-control—you know, smiling on the outside, cracking on the inside. I don't show it, but I am an extremely keyed-up person. I often find myself quivering, and I really have to get a grip on myself." She warned us.

No way Moreuil could keep his grip on her; neither had been faithful. They divorced in 1960. Jean fell next for a diplomat twenty-five years her senior, Romain Gary. She had his son in Spain while he got divorced, then they married. Gary was nuts about her, but the dame made him crazy, so trusting, so naïve. "It made her totally defenseless. In the end, it came between us." Gary was referring to her connections with two black groups, the Malcolm X Foundation and the Black Panthers. Jean spoke at their meetings, loaned them her name, contributed thousands of dollars . . . naïveté combined with movie-star Lutheran guilt. The guilt began back in Iowa when Jean studied the Civil War in school. Horrified by what happened to blacks in America, she became passionate about the civil rights movement. To her parents' dismay, she joined the Des Moines chapter of the NAACP. "Jean, what will people say?" asked her father. "Father, I don't care what they say." They'd have said more about her sexual appetite. There was nothing small-town about it. She was ashamed, but insatiable. Even though the Gary marriage was doomed, he never stopped loving or supporting Jean. And there were rough waters ahead.

Jean fancied herself in love or at least in lust with Hakim Abdullah Jamal, an ex-junkie thief who drifted from the Black Panthers to form the Malcolm X Foundation. Dazzled by him and caught up in the cause, she slept with him, with the Black Panthers' minister of education, and with a Mexican student revolutionary named el Gato. She divorced Gary in 1970 but continued sharing his apartment. When she turned up pregnant, he stood by her. No one was sure who the father might be.

During the revolutionary '60s, the Panthers were a force to be dealt with. The FBI had their every move under surveillance, and Jean's too. J. Edgar Hoover, looking to embarrass her and cheapen her image, had Seberg's pregnancy planted in the *L.A. Times.* Columnist Joyce Haber ran with a blind item: "According to all those 'in' international sources, Topic A is the baby Miss A is expecting and its father. Papa's said to be a rather prominent Black Panther." *Newsweek* ran with the item, saying Jean and Gary may remarry even though her expected child is another man's, "a black activist she met in California." They sued and the magazine settled out of court, but the damage was done. Devastated—or maybe it was the pills—Jean went into labor. Nina was born two months premature. A white baby fathered most likely by el Gato, she died three days later.

Jamal was shot to death by rival black leaders. Jean continued to spin out of control. She married Dennis Berry and broke with the Panthers, but the FBI continued to harass her and monitor her activities. Occasionally she worked. *Lillith* is memorable. During *Paint Your Wagon,* she had an affair with Clint Eastwood; it ended with the shoot.

After six years, she divorced Berry, then dived headfirst into hell. Plagued by multiple emotional problems, diagnosed as a clinical nymphomaniac, her downward spiral gained momentum. Ravaged by dope and booze, tormented by a deep sense of failure, guilt for her rabid sex drive, she burned her flesh with cigarettes, devoured an endless procession of lovers, and repeatedly tried to kill herself. She got grossly fat.

She was in and out of Gary's apartment when she was not with her last love, a young Algerian named Ahmed Hasni. He was twenty; she was forty. They lived in squalor and had terrible quarrels after which she would disappear for days, then call Gary to come get her. But she always went back to Hasni. The attempts at suicide continued. Then, on August 29, 1979, she disappeared again. Cops found her nine days later in the back of her Renault around the corner from her apartment. More than a week in

> *"You forgot to read your fortune cookie. It says, 'You're shit out of luck.'"*
> THE DEAD POOL 1988

the hot sun made it pretty ugly. Her body, bloated and decomposed, was wrapped in a blanket. She'd left a note for her son.

Romain Gary accused the FBI of ruining her life. Bureau director William Webster responded, stating the FBI "now conducts investigations only when there have been charges of criminal conduct." Nothing in the documents made available after Jean's death indicated officials believed the rumors about her. "She was used as an example for others, but the day when the bureau used derogatory information to combat advocates of unpopular causes has now passed." Too little too late for Jean.

Almost a year later, the French press intimated Jean's death may not have been suicide. The levels of alcohol were extraordinary, more than twice what it would take to put her in a coma. There were also barbiturates in her system. But there were no bottles or containers in the car. She'd have had to drink all that, take pills, then walk to the car. Walking seemed pretty doubtful. Could someone have placed her in the car while she was still alive? Gary found that very disturbing. Several months later, he sat at his desk and wrote a letter to his publisher. Then he put a bullet through his head.

Jean liked to serve these as a holiday treat with eggnog. Are you getting this, Mr. Hoover?

Macaroon Peaches

2	tablespoons Burgundy, Sherry, or Kirsch
6	to 8 crushed macaroons
1	can Raggedy Ann peaches
1	cup heavy cream, whipped

Preheat the oven to 350°. Mix the brandy with the macaroons, and fill the peach halves with the mixture. Bake for 10 minutes. Serve hot with whipped cream.

Diane Linkletter

The footsteps of fame can be very deep, so deep it's hard to see your way clear of them. Art Linkletter was a popular TV pitchman and host of a daytime variety show with its trademark spot, "Kids Say the Darndest Things." Seemed like Art had a way with kids. He had five of his own, the youngest his daughter Diane. As she grew up, she struggled to find a bright path in the shadow of her famous father. She loved acting, but reviews always mentioned her father, as if she couldn't have gotten the gig without him. She won a Grammy for Best Spoken Word Record . . . but Dad was on the flip side. She couldn't figure out how to break loose.

Cut to 1969: the peak of the peace-and-love generation. Some kids searching for meaning in life turned to hallucinogenic drugs like LSD to help find answers. According to Art, Diane confided that she had tried it too. She hoped it would help her see her path more clearly, but it had been a "bad trip." And there was more. She was having flashbacks, where the "trip" repeated itself long after the drug had worn off. She was no closer to finding herself and she was torn up about it, consumed; it tortured her. Art really hated that whole scene. And he was loud about it. He lived high on the hog from dough he had made lecturing about the lost generation of kids.

So in October, about three weeks before she hit twenty-one, Diane's parents were in Colorado, where dear old Dad railed against the permissiveness of society with young people. Ironic. Diane didn't feel like she had permission to do anything. She felt trapped in a cell, and the walls were closing in. Alone in her West Hollywood high-rise, six stories above the famed Sunset Strip, Diane watched life pass her by: flower children, beaded, braless, barefoot, greeting one another, smiling, happy, going somewhere. Doubt stalked her: she would never get anywhere on her own . . . never be anything . . . never know herself.

In the wee hours of Saturday, October 4, 1969, about 3:00 A.M., she called her friend Ed Durston, very distraught. He hurried over; they talked for hours. Diane must have felt better because she baked cookies, but Durston says she was touchy and excitable and he could not talk her down. Around 9:00 A.M., she went into the kitchen. Ed later told the police she never came out. Diane's brother Robert said that's when she called him. He promised he'd be right over, but he would not arrive in time. She'd already hung up when Ed came in,

Art cooked up a good story for the press.

and she moved so quickly he had no time to react. In one fell swoop, Diane threw a chair in front of the sink and scrambled up, lunging toward the open window. Instinctively, Ed dived for her. He grabbed the belt loops of her jeans, but as she pushed herself out the window, the loops tore away in his hands. She plunged to the sidewalk and died an hour later from a massive skull fracture.

"We tried and tried but could not fit your fucking name on the cake, Prendergast."
FALLING DOWN, 1993

Police never considered Durston a suspect. From his side of things, they were convinced Diane was despondent, depressed, in a highly emotional state. Durston made no mention of drugs or LSD or flashbacks. But somehow, that's the story that survived: Art Linkletter's daughter tried to fly on LSD. Poor Diane. Even in death, her dad stole the headlines.

"It isn't suicide because she wasn't herself," Art said at a Sunday press conference. "It was murder. She was murdered by the people who manufacture LSD." He said her emotional problems were compounded by intense flashbacks from a previous experience with LSD six months earlier. Now, it seems, despite her bad experience, she had taken it again with dire results. Toxicological tests revealed nothing unusual,

"You're going to have love for breakfast, love for luncheon, and love for dinner. Sweet, sugary, sticky worship. You're going to have a steady diet of it till you're ready to scream—you billygoat!"
IT'S LOVE I'M AFTER, 1937

but Art never caved and crusaded relentlessly against drugs. Diane's memory got lost in the rhetoric.

So what really happened? Was Diane high, or did her parents try to blur the line of suicide to something more acceptable to them: drugs rather than acute unhappiness? Or did brother Robert invent a story to soften the blow to his parents? And here's something else. Ed Durston had two versions of his story: one that ended with the belt loops in his hands, the other that she never returned from the kitchen and when he went to find her, she'd already jumped. But what's really weird is that Durston was involved in the strange death of another woman years later. The body of pretty Carol Wayne was found floating in the very shallow waters of Santiago Bay at Manzanillo in January of 1985. The buxom blonde actress had been the perfect foil in Johnny Carson's "Tea Time Movie" sketches. But the glory days were behind her when she and Durston flew to Mexico. They were seen arguing; he was short on cash. He flew back to L.A. with her luggage and left it at the airport for her to claim the next day. But Carol wasn't coming home. Two days later, her body was found. Local police were never able to question Durston. They conjectured Carol went for a walk alone, slipped on the rocks, and drowned . . . except Carol couldn't swim, hated water, and had no bruises from a fall. So, Ed Durston is the last known person two distraught women ever saw. That's some freaky karma, isn't it?

Diane baked these cookies the night before her death.

Diane's Sugar Cookies

2 dozen

4	ounces (1 stick) soft sweet butter
¾	cup plus 1½ tablespoons sugar
1	large egg
1½	cups flour
1	teaspoon cream of tartar
½	teaspoon baking soda
	Pinch salt

Preheat the oven to 350°. Combine the butter and ¾ cup of the sugar in the bowl of an electric mixer. With the paddle attachment, cream the butter and sugar on medium speed until light and fluffy. Add the egg and beat until smooth. Stir together the flour, cream of tartar, baking soda, and salt. Fold the flour mixture into the butter mixture.

Place the remaining sugar in a bowl. Form the dough into 1-inch balls and roll them in the sugar. Line a baking sheet with parchment paper and put the cookies several inches apart on the pan.

Bake the cookies for 8 to 10 minutes, until golden brown. Allow them to cool for 5 to 10 minutes and then remove them from the baking sheet.

Divine

Harris Glenn Milstead was quite a dish. The movies' most famous 300-pound female impersonator was born in 1945 near Baltimore, Maryland. Let's face it, this bird was always a little screwy. As a teen, he idolized Elizabeth Taylor, and for Halloween dressed up as her character "Gloria" from *Butterfield 8:* a slip, fur coat, and stilettos, the whole tomato. A star was born. "Of course the last thing my parents wanted was a son who wears a cocktail dress that glitters," Glenn later said, "but they've come around to it."

High-school chum John Waters was drawn to Glenn's sense of the bizarre and tacky. In other words, he's a screwball, too. They became lifelong friends and a screen team made in . . . Baltimore. In the '70s, with Waters directing, Divine as leading lady, and a supporting cast of social outcasts and misfits, the pair achieved cult status in a series of films, the most notorious being *Pink Flamingos.* The big payoff: a scene in which Divine eats dog crap. Now that's entertainment. Well, you've gotta admit it's memorable. The

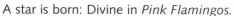

Divine did not live to see
Hairspray's success in movie
theaters or on Broadway as the
Best Musical of 2002.

1980s brought Divine more user-friendly movies like *Polyester* with Tab Hunter, who called Divine "one of my finest leading ladies." Divine's audiences widened . . . along with her girth. People who used to make fun were now fans. This dame was on her way to the middle!

It's only fitting that Divine's biggest success was with John Waters, who, to his credit, became more commercial while maintaining his quirky flamboyance. Critics loved *Hairspray,* a funny, campy tribute to the early 1960s with a wildly nostalgic cast that included Debbie Harry and Sonny Bono. Divine played Edna Turnblad, the hilarious and harried mother of Ricki Lake, a dancer on a Baltimore *American Bandstand*–type show. (Fifteen years later, it became a hot Broadway musical.) No doubt, 1988 was Divine's biggest year, both professionally and personally. At forty-two and 375 pounds, she joked, "All my life I wanted to look like Elizabeth Taylor. Now Elizabeth Taylor looks like me." But the actor, who once ate two whole pies, one quart of ice cream, and a gallon of milk in one sitting, told *Interview* magazine in February: "I don't know why . . . I just get hungry and when I'm hungry, anything that is not nailed down better watch out." She would be dead in a month.

"What am I? A bowl of fruit? A tangerine that peels in a minute?"
SWEET SMELL OF SUCCESS, 1957

Author and playwright Mike Caffey bumped into Divine as Glenn at an ice cream shop about that time. "It was Double Rainbow on Melrose. I saw him in this blue schemata, bald as an egg. I approached him, blathering on about what a fan I was, about how I'd been film chairman at Whittier College and got thrown out of school for showing *Pink Flamingos.* Divine gestured at me with his spoon and cup and scowled, 'Can't you see I'm eating?!?!?' Of course, I laughed because it was such a Divine response, you know? I think he was gone two days later."

In March of 1988, Divine had been hired for her first legit gig . . . a recurring role in *Married . . . With Children* as Katey "Peg Bundy" Segal's mother. This was a network television show going into the homes of millions of suburbanites who would no doubt be seeing Divine for the first time. She'd made it. She was thrilled. It was huge, but so was she.

When she didn't show up on the set for her first day, Divine's agent knew something had to be terribly wrong. He raced to the hotel where he found Divine in bed, dead, wearing a big smile. Official cause: an enlarged heart due to obesity. Doctors now believe death was caused by sleep apnea, when the back of the mouth slips down onto the tongue. (See Cass Elliot.) Friends say Divine had almost suffocated in her sleep on several occasions, but she had always managed to wake up in time. This time, the big sleep won.

The night of her death, Divine chowed down at CITY restaurant. After a full meal, she devoured six caramel flans for dessert, but who was counting . . . apparently not Divine.

Caramel Flan

8 servings

½   cup plus ⅔ cup sugar
3   whole eggs
3   egg yolks
3   cups whole milk
2   teaspoons vanilla extract

Preheat the oven to 350°. Have ready an ungreased 9-inch round or square 1½- to 2-quart baking dish.

Cook ½ cup of the sugar over medium heat in a heavy medium-sized saucepan, stirring almost constantly with a long-handled wooden spoon, until it is melted and turns first golden and then very dark brown, about 5 minutes.

Immediately pour the hot caramel syrup into the baking dish and swirl the pan until it coats the bottom. The caramel will harden at this point and melt again later as the flan bakes.

Gently, but thoroughly, whisk together the eggs, egg yolks, and the remaining ⅔ cup sugar in a mixing bowl until smooth. Gradually whisk in the milk and vanilla. Pour the custard mixture into the prepared dish on top of the caramel. Set the dish in a larger baking pan and fill the larger pan with hot water to come halfway up the sides of the baking dish.

Bake until a knife inserted two-thirds of the way to the center comes out clean, 35 to 45 minutes. The center should still be slightly soft, as the flan will finish cooking after it is removed from the oven. Cool in the water, then remove the baking dish and refrigerate for at least 1 hour or up to 8 hours.

Before serving, run a sharp knife around the edge of the flan to release it. Place a large rimmed serving plate over the baking dish and, using both hands, invert both dishes so that the flan and the liquid sauce unmold onto the platter. Refrigerate again until serving time.

You can also make this flan in individual 8-ounce ramekins. Reduce the baking time by about 10 minutes.

Bibliography

Bosworth, Patricia. *Montgomery Clift: A Biography.* New York: Limelight Editions, 1990.

Cramer, Richard Ben. *Joe DiMaggio: The Hero's Life.* New York: Simon and Schuster, 2000.

Crosby, Bing, as told to Pete Martin. *Call Me Lucky.* New York: Simon and Schuster, 1953.

Crosby, Gary, and Ross Firestone. *Going My Own Way.* Garden City, NY: Doubleday, 1983.

Harmetz, Aljean. *The Making of The Wizard of Oz.* New York: Knopf, 1977.

Israel, Lee. *Kilgallen.* New York: Delacorte Press, 1979.

Jacobs, George, and William Stadiem. *Mr. S.: My Life with Frank Sinatra.* Waterville, ME: Thorndike, 2003.

Kashner, Sam. "Natalie Wood's Fatal Voyage." *Vanity Fair* (March 2000).

Kelley, Kitty. *His Way: The Unauthorized Biography of Frank Sinatra.* Toronto; New York: Bantam Books, 1986.

Kirkpatrick, Sidney. *A Cast of Killers.* New York: Dutton, 1986.

Madsen, Axel. *The Sewing Circle: Hollywood's Greatest Secret: Female Stars Who Loved Other Women.* Secaucus, NJ: Carol Pub. Group, 1995.

Maltin, Leonard, Spencer Green, and Luke Sader, eds. *Leonard Maltin's Movie Encyclopedia.* New York: Dutton, 1994.

O'Brien, Stephen. *Charles Farrell: A Very Remarkable Man.* Copyright © 1997 by Stephen O'Brien.

Palmer, Lilli. *Change Lobsters, and Dance: An Autobiography.* New York: Macmillan, 1975.

Patterson, William T. *The Farmer's Daughter Remembered: The Biography of Actress Inger Stevens.* Philadelphia, PA: Xlibris, 2000.

Pond, Steve. "Phil Spector with a Bullet." *Playboy* 50, no. 6 (June 2003).

Sherman, Vincent. *Studio Affairs: My Life as a Film Director.* Lexington: University Press of Kentucky, 1996.

Shipman, David. *Movie Talk: Who Said What About Whom in the Movies.* New York: St. Martin's Press, 1988.

Slide, Anthony. "The Silent Closet: Homosexuality in Silent Films." *Film Quarterly* (Summer 1999).

Vázquez Corona, Moisés. *Lupe Vélez: A Medio Siglo de Ausencia.* México, D.F.: EDAMEX, 1996.

Walker, Alexander. *Fatal Charm: The Life of Rex Harrison.* New York: St. Martin's Press, 1993.

Wayne, Jane Ellen. *Cooper's Women.* New York: Prentice Hall, 1988.

Williams, Esther, with Digby Diehl. *The Million Dollar Mermaid.* New York: Simon & Schuster, 1999.

Wolf, Marvin J., and Katherine Mader. *Fallen Angels: Chronicles of L.A. Crime and Mystery.* New York: Facts on File Publications, 1986.

Picture Credits

Courtesy of the Bison Archive: 5, 6, 9, 29, 31, 33, 35, 39, 42, 53, 56, 58, 63, 64, 71, 73, 76, 77, 79, 81, 87, 89 (bottom), 90, 91, 92, 101, 102, 107, 121, 122, 123, 125, 129, 130, 136, 137, 142 (bottom), 143, 145, 146 (top), 149, 150, 151, 152, 155, 160, 162, 163, 179, 183, 184, 194, 205 (left), 207, 227, 234

From the author's collection: 7, 15, 21, 22, 23, 24, 30, 37, 47, 54, 61, 65, 87, 89 (top), 108, 110, 115, 146 (bottom), 165, 169, 170, 171, 173, 174, 175, 180, 181, 189, 196, 201, 205 (right), 211, 217, 220, 222, 225, 229, 233, 236, 239, 240

Others: 10: MGM; 43: National General Pictures; 48: Press Association Pictures; 95, 96, 97, 98: Janice Knowlton; 133: MGM/Turner; 141: MGM; 142 (top): MGM; 156: RKO; 159: UPI; 186: Academy of Motion Picture Arts and Sciences; 193: Universal Television; 195: Republic Pictures; 212: Universal

Index

A

Acker, Jean, 124
Albright, Vernon, 71
Alexandra, Czarina, 117
Allen, Steve, 59
Anthony, Barney, 161
Arbuckle, Fatty, 90
Arlen, Richard, 7
Armendariz, Pedro, 157
Arnaz, Desi, 104
Astor, Mary, 129–131
Atkins, Susan, 175
Autry, Gene, 15, 19

B

Badham, Mary, 193
Bakley, Bonny Lee, 194–198
Bankhead, Tallulah, 6
Barker, Lex, 150
Barrymore, John, 8, 60, 80, 129
Belafonte, Harry, 42
Bell, Rex, 90, 92
Bellamy, Ralph, 72
Benchley, Robert, 68
Bennett, Bobbie, 17
Benny, Jack, 19
Bergman, Ingrid, 6
Berkeley, Busby, 66, 217
Bernhardt, Sarah, 117

Berry, Dennis, 231
Black Dahlia, the, 95–100
Blake, Robert, 193–198
Blandick, Clara, 133–135
Bogart, Humphrey, 84
Bolden, Fannie Mae, 218, 221
Bolger, Ray, 134
Bono, Sonny, 109, 241
Bow, Clara, 5–6, 87–93, 131, 161, 205
Brando, Christian, 195
Brando, Marlon, 195
Braun, Harland, 197
Brent, Evelyn, 5
Brody, Adrien, 11
Brown, Mick, 109
Burton, Richard, 36

C

Caldwell, Earle, 197
Campbell, Glen, 109
Campbell, Judy, 166–167
Carmen, Jewell, 62, 64
Carrol, Harrison, 69
Carson, Johnny, 194, 236
Cash, Johnny, 19
Cassini, Oleg, 208
Chandler, Raymond, 57
Chaplin, Charlie, 119
Chasen, Dave, 80
Cheiro, 115–120

Christian, Jonn G., 17
Clark, P. J., 84
Clarkson, Lana, 108, 111
Cleveland, Grover, 117
Clift, Montgomery, 37–40
Clooney, Rosemary, 101
Cobb, Lee J., 166
Cohen, Ellen, 47
Cohen, Mickey, 150, 152–153
Collier, Estella, 173, 176
Colman, Ronald, 72
Columbo, Russ, 6
Cooley, Spade, 15–20
Cooper, Gary, 5–8, 87, 202
Corman, Roger, 108
Corrigan, Tom, 30
Costello, Frank, 138
Crane, Stephen, 150, 152, 202
Crawford, Joan, 7, 83, 141–144
Crosby, Bing, 41–42, 101–105
Cukor, George, 159
Culver, Roland, 218, 222

D

Darin, Bobby, 211–214
Davern, Dennis, 184
Davis, Bette, 142–143
Davis, Ron, 25
Davis, Sammy, 17
De Laurentiis, Dino, 10
Dean, James, 22, 183
Dee, Sandra, 212
Dempsey, Jack, 203
Depp, Johnny, 24
DeVoe, Daisy, 88
Di Cicco, Pat, 63
DiMaggio, Joe, 161–163, 166–168
Divine, 239–243
Doherty, Denny, 48

Dougherty, Jim, 160
Douglas, Kirk, 155
Durante, Jimmy, 61
Durston, Ed, 234–236
Duse, Eleanora, 117

E

Eastwood, Clint, 231
Eisenhower, Dwight D., 207
Eisenstein, Serge, 119
Elliot, Cass, 47–50
Elroy, James, 98–99

F

Fairbanks, Douglas, 119, 123
Farrell, Charles, 71–75
Fields, W. C., 80
Fisher, Eddie, 33–34
Flynn, Errol, 76–80, 207
Folger, Abigail, 174
Fonda, Henry, 30
Ford, Harrison, 12, 21
Ford, Robert, 79
Friedman, Harry, 7
Frykowski, Wojtek, 174

G

Gable, Clark, 17, 39, 74, 104, 138, 210
Gallery, Don, 68
Gardner, Ava, 166
Garland, Judy, 39, 134
Garner, James, 19
Gary, Romain, 230, 232
Gaynor, Janet, 72
Geisler, Jerry, 78–79, 151–152
Gere, Richard, 47
Giancana, Sam, 166–167
Gibson, Donald, 99
Gibson, Margaret, 58

Gilbert, John, 72, 202
Gish, Lillian, 119
Glass, Bonnie, 123
Godard, Jean-Luc, 230
Goldman, Ron, 190, 191
Gordon, Alex, 68
Grant, Cary, 74, 138
Greene, Richard, 208
Guglielmi, Rodolpho, 122

H

Haber, Joyce, 231
Haines, Billy, 143
Haley, Jack, 134
Hamon, Count Louis, 115
Hari, Mata, 117
Harlow, Jean, 87, 138
Harris, Phil, 102
Harrison, George, 109
Harrison, Rex, 208, 218, 220
Harry, Debbie, 241
Harwood, Ronald, 11
Hasni, Ahmed, 231
Hawks, Kenneth, 129
Hayward, Susan, 157
Hill, Virginia, 138
Hoover, J. Edgar, 231
Hope, Bob, 101
Hopper, Hedda, 6, 42, 152
Howe, James Wong, 90
Hudnut, Richard, 126
Hudson, Rock, 38, 179–181
Hughes, Howard, 147, 150
Hunter, Tab, 241
Huston, John, 39

J

Jacobs, George, 166–167
Jamal, Hakim Abdullah, 230

James, Lorenzo, 40
Jolson, Al, 208
Joplin, Janis, 161

K

Kashner, Sam, 185
Kaufman, George S., 130
Keeler, Ruby, 208
Kelley, Tom, 160
Kelly, Gene, 33
Kelly, Grace, 7
Kelly, Patsy, 61
Kennedy, John F., 166
Kennedy, Robert F., 212
Kilgallen, Dorothy, 81–84
Knowlton, George, 96–100
Knowlton, Janice, 95–100
Kollmar, Richard, 82
Kotz, Florence, 166
Krenwinkel, Patricia, 175

L

Lahti, Christine, 21
Lake, Ricki, 241
Lamas, Fernando, 150
Lamour, Dorothy, 101
Landau, Dov, 169
Landis, Carole, 217–223
Lang, Harry, 221
Langtree, Lily, 117
Lansky, Meyer, 137
Lee, Young, 179
Leeds, Lila, 145–148
Lemmon, Lenore, 226
Lennon, John, 49, 109
Liberace, 179–182
Lindsay, Margaret, 63
Linkletter, Art, 233–237
Linkletter, Diane, 233–237

Lombard, Carole, 7, 210
Long, Ray, 57
Luciano, Lucky, 65, 138
Lugosi, Bela, 165
Lumet, Sidney, 21
Lupino, Ida, 63

M

MacLaine, Shirley, 35
MacLean, Faith, 55, 57
Mader, Katherine, 65
Mankiewicz, Tom, 43
Mannix, Eddie, 226
Mannix, Toni, 226, 228
Manson, Charles, 9, 175
March, David, 161
Marple, Cassie, 12
Martin, Dean, 43
Mason, James, 41
Mason, Jeri, 139
Mathis, June, 124
Mathis, Samantha, 25
McCarthy, Joe, 166
McCarthy, Kevin, 38
McFarland, Spanky, 29
McLean, Faith, 54
Medina, Patricia, 208
Melville, Sam, 167
Merriman, Frank, 110
Meyer, Dr. Henry, 116
Mineo, Sal, 169–172
Minter, Mary Miles, 54–57
Mitchum, Robert, 145–148
Monroe, Marilyn, 39, 74, 83, 96, 99, 151,
    159–163, 166
Moore, Clayton, 202
Moorehead, Agnes, 157
Moreuil, François, 229
Morris, Chester, 68

N

Neal, Patricia, 7
Negri, Pola, 126
Nicholas, Czar, 117
Nicholson, Jack, 10
Nilsson, Harry, 49
Niven, David, 207–210
Niven, Primmie, 207–209
Noguchi, Thomas, 186
Normand, Mabel, 53–55
Novak, Kim, 174
Novarro, Ramon, 119

O

Oberon, Merle, 7
Oswald, Lee Harvey, 83

P

Palmer, Lilli, 208, 218, 220
Palmer, Patricia, 58
Parent, Steven, 175–176
Parsons, Louella, 42, 202
Patterson, William T., 42
Peavey, Henry, 54, 59
Penn, Sean, 165
Peters, Ernest, 63–64, 66
Phillips, Michelle, 48–49
Phoenix, River, 21–26
Pickford, Mary, 53, 119
Piott, Jack, 30
Pitts, ZaSu, 61, 67–68
Plimpton, Martha, 24
Polanski, Roman, 9–13, 173
Powell, Dick, 157
Power, Tyrone, 150, 208–209
Preminger, Otto, 229
Presley, Elvis, 118, 183
Prevost, Marie, 142
Provost, Jon, 171, 256

Q

Quinn, Anthony, 41, 44

R

Raft, George, 137
Rambova, Natacha, 126
Ramond, Harald, 202–205
Ranier, Prince, 174
Rasputin, 117–118
Ray, Johnnie, 83
Reagan, Ronald, 17, 19
Reeves, George, 225–228
Reid, Wally, 123
Remarquez, Eric Maria, 202
Reynolds, Burt, 43
Reynolds, Debbie, 33–36
Rio, Jeanne, 180
Roach, Hal, 29, 61, 66, 74
Robson, May, 134
Rogers, Ginger, 74
Rogers, Roy, 15, 17, 30
Romero, Cesar, 208
Rooney, Mickey, 162
Rose, Mason, 78
Rosselli, Johnny, 167
Ruby, Jack, 83
Russell, Leon, 109
Russell, Lillian, 116

S

Sands, Edward, 55
Schafer, Rudy, 68
Schenck, Joe, 66–67
Schlossmen, Stuart, 106
Schmidlapp, Horace, 218
Seberg, Jean, 229–232
Sebring, Jay, 12, 174–175
Shapiro, Robert, 110
Shaw, Artie, 150, 160

Shearer, Norma, 138
Shelby, Charlotte, 56
Sheppard, Sam, 82
Sherman, Vincent, 142
Short, Elizabeth (Betty), 95–100
Siegel, Bugsy, 136–140, 151
Simpson, Nicole Brown, 189–191
Simpson, O. J., 189–191, 197–198
Sinatra, Frank, 74, 82, 165–168
Slatzer, Robert, 205
Slide, Anthony, 72
Sophia, Rose Lenore, 195
Spector, Phil, 107–111
Spector, Ronnie, 109
Steele, Alfred, 143
Stephan, Thad, 95
Stevens, Inger, 41–45
Stewart, Jimmy, 8
Stiltz, Bud, 30
Stockdale, Carl, 57
Stompanato, Johnny, 150
Storm, Gale, 71, 74
Sullivan, Ed, 229
Switzer, Carl "Alfalfa," 29–32

T

Talmadge, Norma, 119
Tana, Dan, 109, 111
Tanner, Deane, 55
Tate, Sharon, 9–10, 173–177
Taylor, Elizabeth, 33–36, 37–39, 239
Taylor, Estelle, 203
Taylor, William Desmond, 53–59
Thorpe, Franklyn, 129
Thurber, James, 52
Tierney, Gene, 208
Todd, Mike, 33–34
Todd, Thelma, 61–69
Tracy, Spencer, 74
Trubshaw, Michael, 208

Turan, Kenneth, 24
Turner, Lana, 138, 149–154
Twain, Mark, 117

Valentino, Rudolph, 121–128
Valli, Virginia, 72
Velez, Lupe, 5–6, 201–206
Vidor, King, 59

Wagner, Robert, 183
Walken, Christopher, 184
Walker, Alexander, 220
Walshe, Pat, 134
Warner, Jack, 78
Warner, William John, 115
Waters, John, 239, 241
Watson, Tex, 175
Wayne, Carol, 236
Wayne, John, 37, 104, 155–157
Webb, Clifton, 122

Webster, William, 232
Weissmuller, Johnny, 202
West, Roland, 62, 66–69
Wheeler, Irving, 217
Whitehead, Mae, 62, 64
Wilcox, Ella Wheeler, 116
Wilde, Oscar, 116
Wilding, Michael, 38
Wilkerson, Billy, 138, 149, 152
Williams, Esther, 219, 222
Williams, Lionel Ray, 172
Wills, Chill, 19
Wilson, Earl, 34
Wolf, Marvin, 65
Wood, Natalie, 183–187, 193

Young, Loretta, 174

Z

Zanuck, Darryl, 73

About the Author

Laurie Jacobson's previous books, *Hollywood Heartbreak* and *Hollywood Haunted,* have solidified her reputation as the reigning expert on Tinseltown ghosts. She has written and produced documentaries, television series, and specials, and she appears regularly on TV and radio. "Wherever they're discussing a scandal, a ghost, or a dead movie star, I'm there," Jacobson says. She lives in Northern California with her own piece of Hollywood history: Her husband, Jon Provost, is TV's beloved Timmy from *Lassie.* They are currently working on his autobiography.